Then with Hermes and Ra...there began the building of that now called Gizeh...that was to be the Hall of the Initiates of that sometimes referred to as the White Brotherhood....

In this same Pyramid did the Great Initiate, the Master, take those last of the Brotherhood degrees with John, the forerunner of Him, at that place...as is shown in that portion when there is the turning back from raising up of *Xerxes*, as the deliverer from an unknown tongue or land; and again is there seen that this occurs in the entrance of the Messiah in this period —1998....

Most Berkley Books are available at special quantity discounts for bulk purchases for sales promotions, premiums, fund raising, or educational use. Special books or book excerpts can also be created to fit specific needs.

For details, write or telephone Special Markets, The Berkley Publishing Group, 200 Madison Avenue, New York, New York 10016; (212) 951-8891.

Edgar Cayce's
Story of
THE ORIGIN AND DESTINY OF MAN

Lytle Robinson

BERKLEY BOOKS, NEW YORK

This Berkley book contains the complete
text of the original hardcover edition.
It has been completely reset in a typeface
designed for easy reading and was printed
from new film.

EDGAR CAYCE'S STORY OF
THE ORIGIN AND
DESTINY OF MAN

A Berkley Book / published by arrangement with
Coward, McCann & Geoghegan, Inc.

PRINTING HISTORY
Coward, McCann & Geoghegan edition published 1972
Berkley edition / September 1976

ISBN: 0-425-09320-4

A BERKLEY BOOK ® TM 757,375
Berkley Books are published by The Berkley Publishing Group,
200 Madison Avenue, New York, New York 10016.
The name "BERKLEY" and the "B" logo
are trademarks belonging to Berkley Publishing Corporation.

PRINTED IN THE UNITED STATES OF AMERICA

20   19

> "In man's analysis and understanding of himself, it is as well to know from whence he came as whither he is going."
>
> EDGAR CAYCE

ACKNOWLEDGEMENTS

I wish to express my indebtedness to the many authors and publishers of volumes upon which I have relied for background material, and for the use of brief quotations therefrom, the latter of which all appear in the Bibliography. I am especially indebted to the Staffs, past and present, of the Edgar Cayce Foundation and the Association for Research and Enlightenment, Inc., for extracts from the files and for reading the manuscript My thanks, also, go to the A.R.E. Press for permission to use three of my former booklets, namely the chapters on *Creation, The Rise and Fall of Atlantis,* and *The Pyramid Builders,* all of which are now out of print. Needless to say, any shortcomings are my own.

L. W. R.

CONTENTS

FOREWORD

Every once in awhile a man comes along who completely upsets the accepted scheme of things. What he says or does challenges our entire concept of the "natural" and the "normal"; a new path is cut through the jungle of the unknown.

Sigmund Freud once said that there are three steps in the history of a great discovery. First, its opponents say that the discoverer is crazy; later, that he is sane but that his discovery is of no real importance; and last that the discovery is important but everybody has known it right along.

Edgar Cayce did not "discover" anything in that sense of the word, but his diagnoses, treatments, analyses, and predictions have done much to bring attention to a new concept of the power of the human mind. He has been called "The Sleeping Prophet", "America's Greatest Psychic", "The Mystery Man of Virginia Beach", "The Man Who Saw Today, Tomorrow, and Yesterday".

Although Cayce died in 1945, his 14,246 "readings" given while in a state of deep sleep or self-hypnosis, are very much alive and gaining new respect. His principle biography, *There is a River*, by Thomas Sugrue, is now in its eighteenth printing, and it first appeared in 1942. Four books on his life and works have been translated into German, French, Japanese and Sinhalese. His contributions to modern thinking in the fields of medicine, theology, philosophy and parapsychology are considerable. Gradually, the Cayce records are becoming recognized as an intriguing, provocative, valid source of information. The historical references dealt with in this volume, controversial to be sure, are nevertheless enlightening. Predictions in national and international affairs, many of which are even now transpiring, are perceptive indeed. They are discussed in Part III.

Cayce (pronounced Casey) had the uncanny ability of putting himself asleep at will and speaking in an authoritative voice on subjects far beyond the range of his normal knowledge. He was not even an avid reader of books. All he needed was the subject to be discussed, or the inquiring person's name, address, and whereabouts, a conductor to make suggestions and ask the questions, and a stenographer to take it all down. Almost every day for forty-two years he went to sleep and answered questions covering an immense range of subject matter. He could do this at any time, any place. There were no darkened rooms, turbans, incense, crystal balls, or paying audiences.

Cayce's mind was apparently able to transcend time and space. A man in Texas wanted to know where he could find an Elliott machine, and was told there were two in Austin. A man in Wyoming was admonished at the beginning of a reading, as his discourses were called for lack of a better name, to "Come back here and sit down!" A man in his New York apartment was given a rare compliment: "Not bad looking pyjamas." Such side remarks were easy to confirm, and they almost invariably proved to be accurate.

A sceptical business man challenged Cayce to trace his steps on the way to his office. The man stopped at a tobacco store and bought two cigars, instead of one as was his habit. He decided to walk up to his office rather than wait for the elevator. Inside, he proceeded to open his morning's mail as usual.

Cayce, asleep in Virginia Beach, Virginia, gave his reading. The unbelieving executive was flabbergasted when he received the report. The clairvoyant had described not only his every move in detail, he had even read his letters!

Cayce's mind apparently could "see" past events as well as the present and future. An unsolved theft of bonds had been committed, and a private detective, stymied without any clues, obtained a reading. Cayce went to sleep and described the thief, saying he had been helped by a woman on the inside; they were staying in a hotel in western Pennsylvania and had the bonds with them. The woman was identified as having a red birthmark on her thigh and two toes grown together on her left foot, the result of a childhood burn.

Excitedly, the detective phoned long-distance to the owner of the bonds, whose response could be heard across the room: "I don't recognize the man, but the woman couldn't be anybody but my wife! She told me she was going to Chicago to visit her sister!"

By the time police reached the hotel, they had checked out, but subsequent readings traced them to Columbus, Ohio, where they were trapped in another hotel. Later Cayce was to say, "I don't like hounding people that way —even if they are guilty."

The one thing he wanted most was for the readings to become "respectable", although persons from all walks of life came to him for help or advice. Among them were a movie producer, an actress, a top steel magnate, a U.S. Senator, a Vice-President of the United States; parents, the sick, the lame, the disturbed. Scientific investigation, which he so desired, drew scant attention. The few qualified scholars who did sit in on readings were as nonplussed as the most unscholarly layman.

The history of Cayce's life and works is indeed one of the most puzzling of our age. His life story sounds like a mixture of the Old Testament and a science-fiction novel. A summary appears in the Appendix. His strange gift of clairvoyance has never been duplicated in modern times, although a few other psychics have proved a measure of ability beyond any doubt. For a period of forty-two years he devoted himself to extrasensory perception in many fields of thought, and verbatim reports of what he had to say are still on file in the custody of the Edgar Cayce Foundation at Virginia Beach. His readings, some 50,000 single-spaced, typewritten pages, constitute perhaps the largest collection of psychic data in the world. A movie on his life and a school, Atlantic University, are in the discussion stage.

Quartered in the same building is the Association for Research and Enlightenment, Inc., which disseminates the information contained in the readings. It is a busy place. Besides the library and offices, there is an auditorium, a therapy department, publications room, press, and a broad, tiled veranda overlooking the ocean. With the steadily growing interest and membership, a staff of 85 workers handles volumes of inquiries, special requests, announcements and literature. Visitors are welcomed and shown about the plant and grounds; everyone, of course, wants to see the readings themselves. To the sceptic there is an appropriate answer; in the words of Abraham Lincoln, "No man has a good enough memory to be a successful liar."

The Cayce records are unique. Twenty million words from an unconscious mind is not a commonplace. If they can be believed, new frontiers wait to be explored. Clairvoyance, clairaudience, dreams, hypnotism, point the way to a better understanding of the history and depth of the human mind and soul. A challenging field lies before man in his search for truth and the meaning of human existence in the earth.

The thesis of this chronicle, based on the Edgar Cayce records, is that man is a spiritual being, that the great continent of Atlantis was a fact, that fleeing Atlanteans settled in many areas of nearby lands, including North and South America, and created high civilizations there, and that these determined, energetic, resourceful people through reincarnation are making their presence felt in radical, forceful ways in America and the world today.

As a famous English scientist once said, I am too much of a sceptic to deny the possibility of anything.

L. W. R.

Tucson, Arizona
October, 1971

PART ONE

STRANGERS IN THE EARTH

CHAPTER ONE

WAS THERE AN ATLANTIS?

In the 2,500-odd "life" readings Edgar Cayce gave, many periods of history, both known and unknown, are commented upon in varying degrees of detail. The Cayce files therefore cast considerable light on the origins and developments of the "mystery races" of the world. These little known, prehistoric people, and they are numerous, have long baffled the best minds of men.

Since only fragmentary evidence of their civilizations exists at this late date, the lack of knowledge is not surprising. What archaeology has learned of their cultures it has had to piece together from scraps of artifacts left here and there by people who apparently were far less interested in history than we are today. It would seem that they simply never went to the trouble to put down, at least in a permanent manner, the chronological events of their day. Or if they did so, the records have been lost.

It is therefore understandable that there is so much speculating, theorizing, and rationalizing about the "mystery tribes". Little else can be done, considering the lack of evidence. Many of the issues involved are necessarily controversial among scholars, and we do not propose to discuss all of them in detail here. Suffice it to say, some of them for our purposes are important, for it is on certain of these very points that the Cayce records throw so much light. Our chief interest, however, is in the colonies of Atlantis and the peoples and areas influenced by that ancient culture in so many parts of the earth, and especially in the Americas.

The reader will readily observe connecting links between civilizations far removed from each other, for all have the common denominator of an Atlantean source or influence. The Cayce readings indicate that the people from the slowly sinking continent of Atlantis emigrated to many widely scattered areas in search of safety, and that their impact was felt in various ways according to the age in which they lived.

Unhappily, official science gives no credence to the Atlantean theory. A few brave scholars have ventured to raise that possibility, but fewer still go so far as to base their case on the premise. The moment such a scientist does so he is likely to be considered outside the fold by his colleagues, and his views cease to be regarded as official or authoritative. Regrettably, this is almost always the circumstance when a new or different hypothesis is put forth, whether in the field of history, philosophy, medicine, theology, physics. Martin Luther was a heretic; Alexander Graham Bell a crackpot; and Robert Fulton a dreamer who was trying to do what everybody knew could not be done. Their names are legion, and they are the ones who have led the way to new horizons. Only the great dare to be different; that is why they are great. They also need to be thick-skinned to weather the professional jealousy and the public ridicule. Still, while we want to be open-minded, we don't want to be so open-minded that the wind blows through.

We will therefore delineate what the Cayce records have to say on the subject after exploring what is considered to be the best and most widely accepted knowledge of it to date. We must bear in mind, however, that tomorrow or twenty years hence, as new findings are made, our factual knowledge may be very different from what it is today. Modern science is not infallible. For centuries men believed and taught that the world is round; now they are certain it is elliptical.

The most convincing thing about Cayce's Atlantean explanation is that it answers questions that so far have largely defied solution. Too, the readings in many instances corroborate points that have never been definitely established, but merely postulated by geology or archaeology. In some cases the information in the readings is simply unmentioned as a possibility, or it may even be diametrically opposed to that which is generally believed. Only time, research, and new discoveries can prove the validity of many of these points.

The readings state that emigrating Atlanteans went in many directions; primarily to the Pyrenees mountains between France and Spain and to North America with the initial cataclysm about 50,700 B.C.; to Central America and Morocco during the second debacle, about 28,000 B.C.; and to Egypt, where they built the pyramids, and Yucatan, Mexico, with the third and final catastrophe in 10,600 B.C. Since these movements were spaced many thousands of years apart, the culture taken to one area in a given period was different from that taken to another at a later period. Because of the Ice Ages, which were intermittent, and earthquakes and volcanic eruptions, drastic land changes were wrought over wide areas of the world. For these reasons, plus the time element itself, little is known of the civilizations today.

We have a classic example of the mystery tribes in the case of the Basques of the Pyrenees Mountains. The Cayce files briefly state that fleeing Atlanteans found their way to those high lands, that they set up a kingdom there, and that their marks may still be seen in the chalk cliffs of Calais.

Today, the modern Basques with their peculiar culture and history smack so much of the Atlanteans that anyone familiar with the story of Atlantis according to the Cayce readings is irresistibly drawn to the conclusion that the Basques are Atlantcan in origin. But there is nothing concrete to prove this. That is the problem we will be faced with throughout our study. Yet the one bright hope is that time and technology will eventually resolve the many questions. One can only wait and see.

From our studies of early man, we will see that there are corroborations as well as discrepancies between science's present knowledge and the Cayce readings. Civilized man has for instance, according to the Cayce files, lived in the earth far longer than once generally believed—some 10½ million years. But man's first large, organized, united effort appears to have taken place about 52,000 years ago, when cooperation was essential in combating the wild beasts still roaming the earth.

Historically, there is now evidence that man lived in Central America perhaps 30,000 years ago, from bits of decorative carved bone found not far from Mexico City. The area also abounds with traditions of ancient visitations from the east, of a great land called Aztlan, and flood stories.

In Peru, the Spaniard Pizarro and his men found 10,000 miles of well-paved stone roads dotted with the remains of numerous inns. This raises the obvious question of what kind of sophisticated people required such roads, and where did they come from? Indeed, there appears to have been a wave of cultural growth that affected civilizations all the way from Egypt to the Andean highlands of Peru in South America and the Midwest of North America. It is apparent that at a certain period in world pre-history—perhaps 10,000 B.C.—striking and sudden changes took place.

American archaeologists have for years been confronted with what appears to be undeniable evidence of trans-Pacific contacts between the Old World and the New.

Leo Deuel, in his book, *Conquistadors Without Swords,* writes:

"Students of American antiquities had of course long been aware of similarities in artifacts, customs, and institutions between the Americas and Southeast Asia, particularly, as well as Polynesia and Melanesia. The Mexican game of patolli can be considered an almost exact replica of the parchesi of Hindu India. The pan pipes in use all over the Andes and into Brazil are virtually indistinguishable from those known to Burma and the Solomon Islands. Star-shaped mace heads from Melanesia resemble those from Peru. The people of Easter Island built masonry of polygonal blocks fitted into each other just as the Incas did. The native sweet potato of South America not only was cultivated in Polynesia before the white man landed there, but bore the same name . . . (An ethnologist) listed forty-nine such parallels between Oceania and South America. Recently, scholars have added still more to them. But how was one to explain these phenomena?"

Deuel quickly discards the "diffusion" theory—the sunken continent of Lemuria, wayward Hebrews and Egyptians—as "unscientific and fantastic". He relates at length Thor Heyerdahl's *Kon Tiki* trip from Peru to Polynesian islands. Yet he states, "Just as Peruvians landed on Pacific isles, Polynesians may well have reached the American coast on several occasions." Their similarities are far too close "to have been independently evolved in the New World", he concedes.

Exactly what happened, how and why and when, science does not know. Yet the architectural monuments of the

Mound Builders, Mayas and Incas demonstrate a relationship and important and unique changes of rather sudden occurrence. Their earthen mounds and stone pyramids are basically similar in design, relating to the pyramids of Egypt across thousands of miles of what is now ocean. Atlanteans, the Cayce files make clear, migrated to that country as well as to the Americas. This correlation of cultures so far removed from each other has long puzzled scholars. It has even raised the question, "Was there at one time a land bridge between Yucatan and Egypt?"

There are intriguing place names to be found in Central America—Azatlan, for instance. And there are such cities as Chol-ula, Calua-can, Zuivan, Colima, Zalisco. Across the ocean in Asia Minor there are similarly Chol, Colua, Zuivana, Cholima, and Zalissa. All this and more points to a common source.

There are also numerous traits which are common to most of the cultures we will discuss. All rather quickly evolved to an agricultural economy, rather than remaining primitive hunters or herdsmen. The sun, their symbol of creative energy, played a significant part in their worship, although the conclusion that the people were in fact sun-worshippers appears to be overdrawn. They were lovers of nature because they lived so close to it and knew they were dependent upon it. The American Indians, for example, recognized the importance of the sun in their lives, and realized that it, like themselves, was the creation of a Supreme Being.

All were highly religious people, believing in one God and living accordingly. Religion was a way of life and the centre of their activities. Cremation was in popular, common usage. All had Flood stories comparable to our own, and many had traditions of a strange, advanced people coming from the East. And legends, we will soon see, are much too lightly taken by modern scholars. Ancient peoples were not given to fiction, and their songs, stories, and ballads handed down from one generation to another were generally rooted in fact. Truth has a way of enduring; untruth lives a short life. To hastily discard these traditions as myths is a reflection of our own present day mentality and morality.

The readings explain many of the enigmas of these early

peoples. The origin of the Incas was from both within and without the country. The mysterious inland movement of the Modern Mayas was obviously due to the rising waters of the Atlantic Ocean. The Mound Builders, former Mayans, were the first to reach Central United States. Recent evidence indicates man lived there as long ago as 7000 B.C.; and the Norseman apparently explored as far as Montana, however unlikely that would appear at first sight.

Also common to these widely separated cultures, and thereby linking them together, was their socio-political system. Practically all were socialist, cooperative or communal societies. What was good for society, the community, came before what was good for the individual, thus leaving no room for self-aggrandizement and the private accumulation of unneeded wealth. There were then an equality and fraternity perhaps unmatched anywhere today.

The issue here, as deep in almost all human questions, is basically a spiritual problem. What does the present state of man dictate? What is he spiritually prepared for? Is he ready to place human rights above property rights? Does he prefer competition or does he prefer cooperation? Of the two, which is most conducive to spiritual growth? These are large questions and one can only philosophize on what man's ultimate answers will be. They are discussed in later chapters.

But of one thing we can be certain; Karl Marx did not invent communism. He borrowed it, separated it from its spiritual source, and declared it to be economically motivated.

We will explore the Old Age up to the fringes of recorded American history, and we shall see how the Lemurian and Atlantean theory answers questions which otherwise remain largely unanswered. Indeed, there is far more evidence in favour of Atlantis than in man's primary entrance from across the Bering Strait, of which there is almost none.

With the rapid advances in oceanography and other sciences, and more importantly, the inquisitiveness and open-mindedness of the younger generation of scholars, it behooves us to explore the latest evidence for the existence of Atlantis. For on that premise rests the burden of our entire concept of history.

Recent developments are causing the raising of some greying, scholarly eyebrows. In October 1968, an Associated Press story by Kenneth Whiting reported: "Evidence is mounting that Africa, South America, India, Australia, and Antarctica were a single great land mass millions of years ago and then drifted apart. Fossils which suggest that the southern hemisphere continents were once a solid mass are helping scientists unravel the geological jigsaw puzzle."

Proponents of the continental drift theory hold that such a land mass broke up and its parts slowly shifted to their present locations. If true, then traces of life found on one would likely be found on the others, along with clues that they existed about the same time.

The routes of glaciers, dents in the earth's crust, belts of minerals and fossils 200 million or more years old lend support to the theory. As glaciers ground over the land they gouged out huge channels and left behind distinctive piles of rubble. Dr. A. R. I. Cruickshank, of Johannesburg, South Africa's Witwatersrand University, said, "From these glacial routes we can deduce the direction of the glacial movement. If we assume that the glaciers radiated from a common centre, then the directions of glacial movements on the various continents, taken separately, do not make sense. But if you swing the continents together, you find a coherent pattern of glacial routes and a common direction in glaciation."

The continents of Africa, South America, India, Australia do roughly fit together. And it all could have happened 200 million years ago. Extravagant as the idea is, the irony lies in the fact that world scientists accept it while pooh-poohing Atlantis, which is hardly more extravagant.

In a recent book, *The Mystery of Atlantis,* Charles Berlitz, grandson of the famous linguist and an archaeologist and pioneer skin-diver, writes: "We can expect archaeological finds relating to the Atlantean culture complex to be discovered on the ocean floor, as, with new and ever more efficient equipment, searchers engage in a variety of underwater investigation. Now for the first time, in the long history of the search for Atlantis, we have the means to get to it and the ability to recognize it."

A noted archaeologist, Dr. Manson Valentine, former professor of zoology at Yale, reported in 1968, 1969 and 1970 that he had made exciting discoveries of Mayan-like temples in Bahamian waters off the coast of Florida: a plaza and sloping walls with steps. The material is a kind of masonry and is definitely man-made. Dr. Valentine believes the pyramid-like structures might be part of Atlantis. They appear to be similar to Mayan temples he has examined in Yucatan, Mexico.

The Bimini Islands, fifty miles off the east coast from Miami, were once part of the Atlantean island of Poseidia, say the readings. On June 28, 1940, the sleeping seer said, "And Poseidia will be among the first portions of Atlantis to rise again. Expect it in sixty-eight and sixty-nine ('68 and '69). Not so far away" (Case # 958–3L–1)

Other mysterious and apparently man-made structures have been sighted under the shallow waters of the Bahamas, Dr. Valentine says. One, a 100-foot pentagon, was found near the site of the temple-like building near Andros Island. He believes more structures will be discovered because large areas of sea bottom are being worn down by changing currents in the Bahamas.

"At least two more distinctive, quite discernible structures have been seen in recent weeks," he said in the spring of 1969. The findings have been confirmed by photographs. The archaeologist and his colleagues applied for clearance from the Bahamian government to begin excavations at the first site near Andros Island. But North American Rockwell Corporation gained exclusive rights.

New finds are a circular structure near Abaco and the pentagon near Andros. "And there are other buildings out there", he says. A pyramid, road, stone wheels, statuary.

Dr. Valentine, who brings impeccable scientific credentials to the venture, places credence in the lost continent theory of Atlantis. He believes the Bahamas finds may be man's first conclusive evidence of a sunken civilization. Yet confusing these discoveries is the fact that a sponge farm was built in one area in the 1920's and later abandoned.

Other researchers have been working in the region of the Bimini Islands. Two of them, Robert Ferro and Michael Grumley, who have also worked with Dr. Valentine, reported their experiences in the recent volume,

Atlantis, The Autobiography of a Search. "It was Wednesday, February 26 (1969), that we found what we found", they write, "whether . . . sea wall or roadbed . . . whatever . . . it had been built by man, and not as an underwater structure . . . We had been pleased to stand and look down through twenty-five feet of bright clear water and see the monumentally unnatural evidence of a very ancient civilization."

Underwater investigation revealed that the stones were aligned forming a wall, usually covered by tidal sands. It has been dated to around 10,000 B.C. by carbon-14 tests.

Another researcher, Count Pino Turolla, found the remains of 40 to 50 stone pillars in a circular formation, some standing, some toppled over. They vary from three to six feet in length and two to four feet in width, of white marble not naturally found in the area. He has photographs of his finds in Ferro's and Grumley's book.

Although as yet no irrefutable hard evidence of the existence of Atlantis has been brought to light, circumstantial evidence continues to accumulate, along with new scholarly adherents. Professor Denis Saurat, a French philosopher, has staunchly defended a theory advanced earlier by an Austrian cosmogonist that Atlantis may have rested in part at least in the Andes Mountains of South America. Ruins of a strange lost city have been found on the banks of Lake Titicaca, located between Peru and Bolivia, and a mysterious 450-mile-long line of fossilized ocean creatures exist high up in the Andes.

In 1952, a German pastor with a historian and a Swiss archaeologist spent four days anchored in the North Sea a few miles off the coast of Heligoland. Over a carefully selected site, a diver brought back reports of a series of man-made walls and ditches just twenty-five feet below the surface but six miles out to sea. The pastor, Jurgen Spanuth, summed up his claim: "During my studies of Egyptian antiquities, I found in the Temple Medinet Habu of Pharaoh Rameses III, the old Egyptian writings and documents which the Egyptian priest used as proof of Atlantis' existence when talking to Solon so long ago. These old Egyptian originals are documents of the highest historical value. They alone contain the key to the solution of the Atlantis mystery . . . The documents contain the exact information of the location of the island country, and also of the king's island which sank during the natural catastrophes. With the help of this information I found the ruins of the sunken fort *exactly on the indicated spot*—and in three different expeditions thoroughly examined it. In upper Egypt, I photographed the inscriptions and wall pictures (one showing a sea battle between the invading Atlanteans and the Egyptian defenders) which served as proof for Solon's Atlantis story."

In 1966, a Greek-American scientific expedition spent two weeks on the Aegean Island of Santorini. They returned to Athens full of hope. Dr. James Mavor, of Woods Hole Oceanographic Institution in Massachusetts, who headed the team, reported: "Although we have not discovered Atlantis, there are shreds of evidence, which, if put together, point towards a confirmation of the theory that the lost continent should be identified with the Minoan Empire which ruled the Aegean Archipelago and Crete about 1500 B.C." The group continued its search and uncovered what some believe to be Atlantis, although the date is much too recent.

Other scientists have recently begun to give weight to the Atlantean theory. Maurice Ewing, of LaMont Observatory and a leading authority on the Atlantic ocean bottom, is one. His expedition found that an abrupt change took place about 11,000 years ago in the Caribbean Sea from cold water type plants to warm water types, and 17,000 years before that there were widespread earth changes. Other U.S. oceanographers, Walter Sproll and Robert S. Dietz of the Environmental Science Services Administration, have theorized that Australia and Antarctica are parts of a once super-continent. They constitute the lands of the continental drift theory—broken off chunks of the present continents, they believe.

Recent discoveries reveal the exclusive presence of fresh water plants in the sedimentary material along the mid-Atlantic submarine ridge, indicating it was once above water. In the Azores, a prominent Russian geologist, Dr. Maria Klionova, reported to the Academy of Sciences of the USSR that rocks dredged up from depths of 6,600 feet showed evidence of having been exposed to the atmosphere about 15,000 B.C. Similar evidence came to light as long ago as 1898, when pieces of lava were found to have a glassy structure, meaning it could only have solidified in the open air.

The ocean bed is known to be unstable, rising and falling unpredictably. Volcanic islands have suddenly appeared, disappeared, and reappeared. Depth soundings in the Straits of Florida show a series of bumps intriguingly about the size of houses, two thousand feet below the surface. And recent research reveals the sinking of large land areas near Florida and the Bahamas at least eight thousand years ago.

So the circumstantial evidence in favour of the Atlantean theory continues to accumulate. Men of science are beginning to give more credence to the idea. There is every reason to believe that modern technology can eventually resolve the problems and questions that to date have proved insoluble.

We can therefore look forward to some exciting revelations in the years immediately ahead. For the Atlanteans were a unique people, and they may be influencing American life today in unexpected ways.

But let us begin at the beginning.

CHAPTER TWO

CREATION

When man first began to think, he began to ask questions. Among his first questions were: "Who am I?" . . . "Where did I come from?" . . . "What is the purpose and meaning of life?" . . . "Why do we die—where do we go?" But man's capacity for asking questions has always been greater than his ability to answer them, and this has served as an intellectual prod—having its role in mental development. Man has not yet satisfied his thirst for knowledge, although deep within himself—unknowingly—lie the answers.

Over the centuries the mystery of man's origin and that of the universe has provoked the imagination, and the world's greatest thinkers have devoted themselves to such questions, each building his theories from the work of those who have gone before. The nature of man and the universe are therefore two of the principal problems of philosophy. Did the earth come into being through an act of divine creation? Or is it the result of an accidental evolution and growth? Of what basic substance is it made and why is it so diverse? What role does man play in the universe? Is he a mere speck of unimportant matter in an ungoverned, unlimited expanse of space? Or is he the crowning achievement of a Supreme Intelligence?

The first known philosopher to attack these problems was Thales, who lived in Ancient Greece about 600 B.C. He decided that water must be the original stuff of which man and the world were made. For when it was frozen it was solid, and when heated it was mist and air. Therefore, he reasoned, everything came originally from water and must eventually return to water. Thales never knew how close he came. If he had meant and used the word *spirit* instead of *water* he might one day yet be lauded for his vision and inspiration. But he didn't; and now Thales is all but forgotten.

A little later another Greek thinker, Anaximander, suggested that the universe was a living mass filling all space.

He called it the "infinite" and said that it contained motion. This was a step forward, even though some of Anaximander's other ideas were strange ones indeed.

This line of thought paved the way for the *Atomists,* another group of early Greek philosophers. They agreed with some of their predecessors that change and diversity were due to the mixing and separating of tiny units; but said that these units or atoms were not as different in substance as previously thought. Each atom has motion, they declared, and by uniting in different ways and numbers matter was formed. The atoms themselves never changed but were eternal and minutely small. Changes in form of life were accounted for by the coming-together of atoms; conversely, death resulted from the separation. Although some of their conclusions were far afield, the *Atomist's* general concept may be viewed as another move in the right direction.

While the *Apologists* were attempting to defend and reconcile the Genesis version of creation with philosophy, the *Sceptics* on the opposite side were busy refuting their conclusions. This school of thought, founded by Pyrrho in about 300 B.C., contended that all so-called explanations of the nature of the universe were futile and a waste of time. It was in favour of giving up the search in despair; man did not know, could not know the nature of things. All man knew was what he could see and measure, and he should accept nothing else. Such a pessimistic point of view offered little in place of what was rejected.

It was Philo, the Jewish philosopher who lived during the time of Jesus, who first attempted to merge the Mosaic Bible version of creation with Greek philosophy. He taught that there were many powers or spirits which radiated from one source, God; and one of these, called the "Logos" was the creator of the world. Further, he taught everything in the universe is an expression or copy of an idea in the mind of God.

His teachings had a profound influence on religious writers, both Jewish and Christian. The early Christian scholars quickly identified Philo's *Logos* with Jesus, who was the Christ, the Word—the agent of God in the creation of the world.

Then came Plotinus, in the third century A.D. His views

were much like those of Philo. He concluded that from a
pure God came beings, or emanations, flowing as light
flows from a sun, without diminishing it. The further the
light is from the source, the dimmer it becomes. At the far
extreme is matter or darkness—the earth and fallen man
—but between God and matter is the great soul-mind.

Modern theories of the origin of the universe fall chiefly
into three groups. The first is materialistic *Monism,* which
maintains that the world is just an accident; it is purely
mechanical, self-existent, eternal—underived from and independent of any external cause. By a gradual process of
evolution from a simple state, and by chance alone, it has
attained its present complexity. The idea is not new but was
first taught by Epicurus in 306 B.C. This is "Evolutionism",
and since it never quite explains what the original "simple
state" was, or how it came into being, the theory only
defers the problem rather than answers it.

A second modern view asserts that the world is derived
from an extraneous cause, either by emanation from or
evolution of a Divine Being. This is *Pantheism.* Spinoza,
who lived in the seventeenth century, went so far as to declare boldly that everything in the universe is the manifestation of God, and that all existence is embraced in one
substance; God, or Nature. Evil exists only for finite minds,
he said, and dissolves when seen as part of the whole.
Spinoza was thrown out of the synagogue for his views;
he was called "intoxicated with God". Nevertheless, he
offered some sober and provocative ideas.

A third modern belief is one of outright creation of the
world from nothing. This is *Creationism,* and is the traditional religious viewpoint. God, as the Creator, is indivisible
and therefore emanation is an impossibility. Further, the
universe is not self-existent but was created, and not from
some primordial substance. The big-bang theory of modern
science is corroborative, and the two are slowly moving
close together. Matter is atoms, atoms are energy, energy
equals spirit, spirit is of God.

Christian ideas about the origin of the soul subdivide
into two classifications. *Traducianism,* first taught by Ter-
tullian in about A.D. 200, is the doctrine that the soul is
created from other souls or physical beings in the same way
and at the same time the body is formed from other bodies

at conception. *Creationism* holds that God creates a new soul for each body. For the church, the question has never been satisfactorily resolved. Even Augustine and Luther were undecided about the nature of the soul. The traditional philosophy of the church maintains that the soul is created at the moment when it is infused into the new organism.

Among the early Greek thinkers, Plato believed in the pre-existence of souls and their subsequent incarceration in bodies. A little later Philo and Origen, who also was excommunicated for his views, taught the Divine source of the soul and also its pre-existence and transmigration from spirit to matter, matter to spirit.

Indian philosophies, Brahminism, the world's oldest religion, and Buddhism, make a distinction between body and soul (Dualism) and teach that physical life is merely a transitory episode in the evolution of the soul. A few Indian sects believe, however, that incarnation takes place in the animal kingdom as well as in the human. The Jewish Cabala and the Gnostics (a mixture of early Christian and Jewish elements) taught much the same ideas, except that the reincarnation of the soul was confined to the human race.

The ancient Israelites were divided into two main schools of thought. The Pharisees believed in a spiritual existence and in immortality, including the pre-existence of the soul and its incarnation from spiritual to human life. The Sadducees were the Materialists, denying immortality and all spiritual existence. Men were born, they lived, they died; that was all, they said.

Although modern science has propounded many theories as to how some primeval gaseous substance evolved into the present harmony of the universe, it bestows no such attention upon the existence of the soul. If it exists at all, it says, it is unproved and unidentified—and, *ipso facto,* unlikely. In recent years, however, startling advances have been made in this very field (Parapsychology), although the psychic powers of man have not yet been officially related to the soul or spirit in man by name.

Thus scholars have long struggled with the problems of the nature of man and the universe. They have in turn upheld, denied and compromised with the Mosaic Cosmogony as briefly outlined in that remarkable book, the Bible. Throughout the whole debate, the Genesis version of creation still stands firm and unrefuted. Because much of it is symbolic rather than literal, its profound depth and breadth—its esoteric meaning—escape the minds of those who would confine it to a literal interpretation.

The Edgar Cayce readings generally follow the Mosaic pattern in principle if not in detail. This is to be expected, since detail is lacking almost entirely in the Genesis account. The Cayce readings, however, throw a great deal of light on some of the missing elements. More than that, they supply sound and convincing explanations for shadowy passages that have long remained in the realm of speculation. Out of this wealth of material in the readings emerges a version of creation that is both comprehensive and understandable. Indeed, here is a simplified description of a complicated series of events that normally are almost beyond the reach of the human mind.

Much of the best knowledge of man is corroborated in the Cayce readings; but there are also areas of disagreement, especially as to the modern materialistic concepts of creation. This is not surprising, since its adherents not only disagree among themselves but reject any ideas of a spiritual concept. Their arguments are almost altogether theoretical because so little concrete evidence exists. Yet both schools of thought could be right.

In the theory of evolution we have a paradox: The *evolutionists* say man evolved from the animal; *theology* says he is the offspring of God. The readings say both, in a sense, are right: the soul of man is indeed the child of God, and the physical body was patterned after, and in one branch, evolved from the animal kingdom. The earth, too, was both created and has evolved. But the "missing link" has not been found because there is no missing link.

Man is believed to be from three to ten million years old, and the dates are far from certain. The oldest evidence, a jawbone and tooth found in Kenya, dates to only five million years, and this recent find is three times the age previously believed by most scholars. Gradually, the veil of mystery is being pushed back.

In a sense even the sceptic is right; man actually knows little for certain about the nature of creation; but what he has reason to believe probable is all-important as a guide for his ideals, his patterns for growth. One can only consider, select and accept that which has the ring of truth for one's self. The concepts in the Cayce records appear to be as solidly founded on reason and plausibility as any yet imagined by man. And they not only tell *how,* they tell *why*.

What follows then, is the story of creation that emerges from the readings. It contains no outside sources and little speculation; in one or two instances certain assumptions and interpretations, which the material seems to support, appear advisable for the sake of continuity and completeness.

From the Cayce Records

In the beginning was the Spirit; a vast sea of mind-force, of discerning energy, occupying all space, all time. Omniscient, omnipotent, omnipresent, this was the source of all; the First Cause, the Universal Force. This was the Whole, the essence of life, the I AM THAT I AM. This was the eternal God.

The mind of God embraces the total life energy, for all in its elemental form is One. All time, all space, all power and matter essentially are one and are based on the force of attraction and repulsion, the positive and negative law around which the universe revolves. The movement, the vibration of this atomic structure is the manifestation of the Creator. During its nebulous activity the gathering of positive-negative forces becomes the *creative* power. Atoms, molecules, cells, and matter change; but the essence, the spirit, does not change. Only the form of manifestation changes, not its relationship to the First Cause.

The *second cause* was desire: desire for self-expression, desire to create, desire for companionship. The Spirit moved, and by moving Itself out of Itself created a separate vibration; a separate manifestation. Thus, into this sea of peaceful and harmonious vibration came one *Amilius,* the Light; the first expression of divine mind, the first manifestation of the spirit, the first Son who emanated in spirit from the Source as a beautiful thought is created or as an idea is born. This was the first creation.

Amilius by necessity was endowed with free will and reason, otherwise he would remain *of* the Whole, *at the will* of the Whole. Although a part of the Source and aware of his identity with the Source, he was a separate entity and conscious of his own individuality while still one with the Creator in spirit and purpose.

It was Amilius who fostered the coming of other soul entities into this electro-spiritual world—for all souls were created in the beginning; none were created later. With their free will and reason, they existed as children in a state of perfection, in full accord with the divine will of their Source. These numberless, sexless manifestations of the spirit were the perfect offspring of a benevolent Father, and enjoyed a truly spiritual life in a truly spiritual world. Wholly attuned to the Supreme Will as was Amilius, they were the companions of the Father as they were intended to be; a part of the Whole yet aware of being separate and independent entities.

Since they possessed free will, each entity's first thought, first reaction and first expression were slightly different from those of all others. Thus each individual idea and each realization or motive became a part of the entity. Thought upon thought, experience after experience, each of these unembodied spirits built its own peculiar individuality and character. The activity of the spiritual entity thus became its soul-record. That which it thought it gradually became.

Every thought and every deed registered not only on the entity's soul but on the skein of time and space, or the Akashic Records. This is the "Recording Angel" or the "Book of Life". Nothing escapes it. Every vibration from the beginning is permanently recorded on the stream of time and space.

But not for long did the will of the souls remain the will of their Source. They began to experiment, fascinated with the power of their own creative individuality. Desire and self-aggrandizement gave birth to the destructive—that which was opposed to goodness, the opposite of God's will. By magnifying their own will and independence, the selfishness of the ego came into being. It was this turning away from God's will that brought about the downfall, the separation, the end of the state of perfection. This was the Revolt of the Angels, or the Fall of Man.

When souls turned from God's will to their own they separated themselves from their spiritual home, their natural home, for a long time to come. The link was severed by their own choice and only by their own choice could it be reforged. Soon there was no turning back; the perfect state which was their birthright was already too difficult to attain. A self-created evolution was under way. They fell away further and further from the Divine Will until there was no hope for a retreat—a return to their natural abode.

Amilius realized what was happening. A plan was conceived whereby a means of escape was devised from the predicament into which the "lost" souls had fallen. By intervening he accepted voluntarily the burden of the world to come—a task almost overwhelming in its magnitude. This was the first of many sacrifices.

In accordance with the plan, materiality came into being; for matter was essential in order to demonstrate physically the *separation from spirit*, so that the souls might become aware of their fall, although the earth was not created solely for man. The solar systems, the planets, and the earth took form, created by the same thought vibrations and the same life-essence emanating from the mind of God. The poles—the positive and negative around which the world revolves—were the keystones. The atom, made up of negative electrons revolving with positive protons, was the building block. Every atom, every cell is a world in itself and motivated by the same life-giving spirit; not the Creator but the manifestation of the Creator.

The Cosmos was built by and upon the principles which became known as music, arithmetic and geometry; harmony, system and balance. By changing the rate of vibration—the wave-length and the frequency, so to speak—varying movements, patterns, forms and substances came into being. This was the beginning of the law of diversity which supplies endless designs for the universal pattern. Upon this law are based the great divisions in force and matter.

Each design carried inherently within itself its own plan of growth and evolution, which corresponds to the sound of a musical note. Notes unite to make chords; chords become phrases; phrases turn into melodies; melodies intermingle around and between each other to make a symphony. Back and forth the mind of God played upon the universe; unlimited within the scope of imagination of an all-creative Spirit.

All matter moved and changed, assuming its design according to its own vibration and maintaining its activity by the law of attraction and repulsion, the positive and the negative. Everything that came into being was an aspect of mind—the Spirit of the Creator.

All matter contains spirit, and is electrical in function, manifesting in different forms because of varying rates of vibration or speed. Every condition that exists in the material plane has its counterpart and its pattern in the cosmic or spiritual plane. All force is one force. Things spiritual and things material are the same in essence although different in manifestation or expression.

The earth is only an atom in the universe of worlds. The solar system comprises other dimensions or other states of consciousness of existence. Although each dimension has its own set of laws, the same force governing the earth rules the planets, the stars, the constellations, for all are held in space by the same law of attraction and repulsion. The earth represents the third dimension, the testing laboratory for the entire system. The other planes—Mercury, Mars, Venus, Jupiter, Saturn, Neptune, Uranus—were to play their part in the plan of evolution for the soul, although in a way somewhat different from that later supposed.

"The earth plane, first a mass of vibrating heat from which arose a seething mist, settled itself as a companion world in the universe of worlds. As it began its natural rotation, it slowly moved closer to the sun, from which it receives its impetus for the awakening of the elements that give life in its various forms." (Case # 364-6)

The laws of creative forces are universal. The first is the law of Love, the second the law of propagation, the third the law of evolution, or growth and development. Thus the spirit of God, the Creative Force, had moved over the face of the earth, and out of chaos came the beauty of raw nature in all its glory.

Said Cayce: "The mind of God embraces the one total life energy with its universally evolved portion called mind, in all its forms, all its stages of development, and all of its self-conscious, individual viewpoints, including ourselves. Yet while in the physical form we possess not the Creator's kind of mind, but rather the kind that mind becomes in materiality." (Case # 792–Ca)

"The First Cause was that the created would be the companion for the Creator; that it, the creature, would by its manifestations in activity of that (which was) given unto the creature, show itself to be not only worthy of but companionable to the Creator. Hence every form of life that man sees in a material world is an essence or manifestation of the Creator; not the Creator but a manifestation of the First Cause.

"Then a soul—the offspring of the Creator—(when) entering into a consciousness which becomes a manifestation in any plane or sphere of activity, is given free will for its use of those abilities or qualities or conditions in its experience. And it will demonstrate, manifest and show forth what it reflects in its activity towards that First Cause." (Case # 364–Sd–1)

To Amilius was given the keeping of the earth-sphere. The mineral, plant and animal kingdoms were thriving long before man entered this plane. They were governed by immutable laws already set in motion. Souls still in the spirit were attracted by matter and came to the new outer realms in large numbers. The earth was only one of many spheres that came into their paths and to which they were drawn.

Those souls, still in the spirit, who were attracted to the earth plane observed the various forms of animal life and the fleshly ties. They hovered about it, viewing the abundance of growing things in the slowly cooling and tropical earth. They saw the fruit of the land and wanted to taste it; they observed the sex life of the animals and wanted to experience it. Since desire impelled them to seek expression in matter, they partook more and more of the material, becoming eaters of, feeders upon their physical surroundings.

Since souls were also self-conscious viewpoints possessed of God and capable of being that which God is, they played at creation—imitating the Creator. Thus they became absorbed with their own creative powers, with which they had been endowed from the beginning, and they mimicked the beasts of the fields and the fowls of the air, dreaming up ideas of bodies it would be pleasant to inhabit.

Thoughts are deeds, and these desires eventually materialized; for from the beginning the resources of all creation have been available to man. The forms so conceived were at first merely in the nature of thought-forms or visualizations, made by pushing themselves out of themselves in whatever manner desired—much in the way of the atom which, when split, eventually forms two more complete atoms; or as the growth of the amoebae in the waters of a stagnant pool, which multiply themselves again and again. As the gratification of their carnal and material desires took shape, however, the forms hardened or congealed into matter itself and took on the colour of the environment, much as a chameleon adapts itself or takes on the colour of its surroundings.

The mentality of the soul was its predominant activity, or direction of growth. The fact that the mental was constantly seeking expression in and becoming attached to the material necessitated a division of the mind-force. This resulted in the three phases of thought-process: the *Conscious* mind which gives direction to the building-up, use and control of matter; the *subconscious* or unconscious which is the storehouse of memory, the inter-between; and the *superconscious* which is devoted entirely to the soul-mind.

These are not three distinct minds but rather are the functions of *one mind at three different levels*. Between the conscious and the superconscious there appears to be a constant war, or working at cross-purposes. Yet in the end the superconscious must be the victor.

As souls used and abused their privileges, the highest and the lowest applications of divine forces were made. The few who sought to know the way were given guidance, as it has always been given; the masses deliberately turned away, seeking fulfilment of their own desires. These became entrapped.

Chaos resulted not only from the forms taken but from the misapplication of spiritual powers. The male and female came into being. This was the separation of the sexes, the division of the nature of "man" into positive and negative forces.

The first female was called *Lilith,* the forerunner of Eve, and a conglomeration of monstrosities emerged. The Cyclops, the satyr, centaur, unicorn and various forms mentioned in mythology, having animal bodies and human heads, came into existence. Thus the souls who had been hovering about, influencing and directing, inhabited bodies which were projections of their own mental creations— and propagated a race of monstrosities.

Their bodies were their own creations, not God's. These were the *daughters of men, the giants in the earth,* of the Old Testament. So a weird, corrupt state of existence came into being, but it was the beginning of a new period of evolution for the soul—the long struggle for spirit's conquest over matter.

The monstrosities roamed the earth and mixed with the animals. Sex was the determining factor, as symbolized by the serpent. Through their offspring souls were being born again and again into a prison of matter from which they could not extricate themselves. Trapped in these grotesque bodies, man as such was drifting further and further away from his Source, the harmonious existence in peace and love which had been his. This he had wilfully discarded for the selfish gratification of the carnal; and he had accomplished it by the spiritually destructive use of *creative* powers for *self.* This was the Original Sin of man.

Only in the earth did souls take on matter and become physical. In other planes and realms—other states of consciousness—the plan for evolution of the spirit varied. Only in the physical, three-dimensional plane does the transition from one plane to another necessitate the process called birth and death. The soul, the spirit of God in man, has been immortal from the beginning. It is not born and does not die, for souls are as corpuscles in the body of God, the Whole.

Amilius, with the aid of spiritual-minded soul entities from other realms—the "sons of the Most High"—intervened in this misshapened evolution which earth-man had created for himself. From among the various physical forms on earth a body was patterned which most perfectly fitted the needs of man. This was a body that would help, not hinder, in the struggle for at-one-ment (atonement) with the Maker.

By his own choice, Amilius himself descended into matter and became Adam, man as flesh and blood, the first of the perfect race, the first of the Sons of God as opposed to "Daughters of Men", the freakish offspring of the Mixtures. This was the reason for the admonishment to *keep the race pure,* for "the Sons of God looked upon the daughters of Men and saw them as being fair." (Gen. 6:2)

Adam was an individual but he was also more; he was the symbol of the whole race of man, the five races. Eve was created as the ideal helpmate for Adam, because of the division of man's spiritual nature into positive and negative. Thus Eve was also the symbolic "other half" of man's nature in all races. This was the last of the important creations.

In woman, the negative and receptive was expressed; the positive suppressed. In man, the positive and active was expressed and the negative suppressed. For at first the Sons of God, the souls, were androgynous, combining male and female as one. The first companion, Lilith, was a projection into the animal world—a means to an end, for the satisfying of desire which had entered. With the turning-back to the Creator's plans and the turning-within to creative impulses, the creation of Eve was made necessary as a helpmate and a balance in the long struggle back to God which was to ensue. Eve was created by God and drawn in an instant from the soul-entity already in existence. "God said, Let there be life," and there was life.

Through Eve, the perfect complement to Adam, there was the channel for reproduction of the perfect race. Cain was born of physically perfect parents. Adam and Eve, with their contemporaries, were special creations and not evolutions from that which had already been created. Man did not descend from the monkey.

Everything in the earth had been prepared for the coming of man. The immutable laws of nature were established for his life and sustenance. Through the law of relativity, the positive and the negative, man and woman experience earth; night and day, hot and cold, good and bad—all realized through the five physical senses via the reasoning of the mind.

Yet always man retains—even unknowingly—the sixth, seventh and eighth senses. These are the psychic or extra-sensory factors of the soul which have gradually receded into the background as man has entered more and more into matter.

The projection of the perfect race into matter occurred not only in the Garden of Eden—which the readings say was in Iran and the Caucasus—but in five different places in the earth at the same time.

These five occupations in the world represented the five physical senses which are to be conquered before spiritual perfection can again be attained. There were 133 million souls in the earth at this time. The white race was in Iran, the Caucasus area along the Black Sea, and the Carpathian Mountains of Central Europe. The yellow race was in what was later to become the Gobi Desert of East Asia. The black race was in the Sudan and upper West Africa. The brown race was in the Andes and Lemuria, the continent lying then in the area of the Pacific Ocean. The red race was in Atlantis and America.

The environment and climatic conditions determined the colour of the race. For all peoples, regardless of colour, were of one blood and members of the "perfect" race. Colour of the race merely adapted man to the conditions which were to be met, and symbolized the chief attribute of the people of that race. In the white race, sight or seeing was predominant or emphasized; in the red, feeling or emotion; in the yellow, hearing; in the black, gratification of the appetites; and in the brown, the emphasis on the sense of smell.

The Jews, as a people, developed at a much later date. The Egyptians also came later, as a result of the mixture of red, black, and white races, in about 10,000 B.C.

The continent of Atlantis was the most important land area of the world and the centre of the first civilization. With the second influx of souls—i.e., the coming of the perfect race, some 10½ million years ago—a new era was to begin in the evolution of man in the earth.

The Atlanteans were a peaceful people and made rapid progress in utilizing the resources of nature. Natural gas and fire were among the first discoveries. In the years ahead they were to build a civilization superior in many ways to any fashioned since.

Division of the forces of mind took place during the first thousand years of the occupation of the earth by the perfect race. By this division part of the mental forces related to the material, and part to the spiritual. It occurred as man emphasized less and less the divine aspect of his nature, became less and less aware of that from which he came. For man recognized that he was a part of what was about him, and he acknowledged the oneness of all matter and force, but he relied more and more on the physical mind with its carnal interpretations. As time went on, only dreams, prayer, and religion remained to remind him of his divine origin. Desire led him to accept things which he instinctively knew were not true; he mingled with the monstrosities and produced the "mixtures"—half animal and half human. Finally, he put ego of self above everything else, "And it repented the Lord that he had made man on the earth and it grieved him in his heart." (Gen. 6:6) The Bible gives an account of the flood, which occurred about 28,000 B.C., and in Atlantis it resulted in the submergence of many large islands. Lemuria too, vanished into the Pacific Ocean.

Yet even in those days, as in all ages, there were men who were able to attain to such a high consciousness of the Creator that it was not necessary for them to pass again through the earth plane. For "even in that day did they call upon the name of the Lord". . . . And "Enoch walked with God, and he was not; for God took him." (Gen. 5:24) A few souls return to the earth plane by choice, the many by law.

From time to time individuals were raised for specific purposes, and as the cycle continued, again and again there rose certain souls manifesting in a "more beneficent, more magnificent and noble manner" to show the way for man. There has always been direction for those who seek the light, the way to become one again with the Creator. Throughout man's many and varied periods of development, his progress has accelerated or retrograded, or remained stationary, in proportion to the exercise of his *will* toward good. Thus in each man's development the first to be conquered is self. Like begets like, for this is part of the universal law. Putting it another way, the mind of man itself, in its total functioning, must be unified and harmonized if he is to remember and accept his divine origin, his inheritance.

There have been almost as many variations in the use of mind-force as there are individuals. What a soul fed upon, dwelt upon, became its means of development or retardation; for good and evil were expressed according to motives and the use made of motives. The people of Atlantis were to pass through the same stages of development as did the other races in other lands; but their progress was to be more rapid, materially if not spiritually.

Thus through the Christ spirit, the Holy Spirit in Adam —in man as a race—a way was prepared for the conquest of the world; the conquest of spirit over matter, good over evil. Hence, Adam, as an individual as well as a group (Adam means man), started humanity on the long journey back to the state of being worthy of and companionable to the Creator. It was to be a long, weary journey, for men are strangers in the earth.

In the 1930's Edgar Cayce gave a series of lectures on the creation story in the Scriptures. This is the gist of what he said.

In the Bible, the writer of Genesis had the task of explaining infinite happenings in finite words, understandable to finite minds in principle if not in method. The first chapters deal with the period *before* and *during* the five-point projection of the Christ Soul, Amilius, into the earth plane.

The book of Genesis is supposed to have been written by Moses with Joshua, and was evidently done with the idea of giving the people of Moses' time a concept of what took place in the beginning of man's advent into material consciousness.

The Book of Job, written by Melchisedek, is an account of the Son into whose hands the earth was committed and who passed through the trials in the flesh so that he might become the deliverer of mankind.

The Bible is primarily an esoteric book, a symbolic book.

Genesis is the story of creation compressed into a few short verses. Symbols and personifications are used in an earthly setting to convey ideas behind occurrences throughout the universe, in the spirit realm, and in the human body itself.

It is in the second chapter of Genesis, in the story of Adam, that the real history of man, as man, begins. This is not a recapitulation of what has gone before. Where the first chapter of Genesis speaks of man the spirit, the second chapter deals with the coming of the perfect race and man's physical tenure on earth, "for there was not a man to till the ground" (Verse 5). The earth was complete in itself, with the ability to supply everything necessary for the reproduction of itself.

As a result of the creation of the sixth day the earth became occupied with souls who had projected themselves into matter, interested in the physical evolution taking place in the earth—and not yet conscious that they were thus separating themselves from the image in which they had been made. A perfect, physical man had to be created as a separate creation, in order that there might be a comparison for the souls who had projected themselves into animals and produced monstrosities. Man, perfect physical man, created in Genesis 2:7, would be a physical counterpart of that spiritual creation expressed in Genesis 1:26. The material man created was made in the image of God, in that he was formed of the dust of the ground, i.e., the human body is chemically composed of all the elements in the earth.

As the souls were created in the beginning, they were neither male nor female, but both, a complete whole. The soul itself has no sex, and it takes on the positive or negative expression when it comes into materiality, according to its development and its purpose to be accomplished.

The time arrived when Adam, too, was divided as in other phases of creation. Eve was created to complete Adam's expression as the example for others. Adam had already been made complete, so it was necessary to take from his physical body the negative force which would be expressed by Eve. This does not mean that Adam's soul was split, but that out of his body was taken negative force through which another soul manifested as Eve. They were what we might call twin souls. Each soul is complete in itself, but in relation to one another, man is positive and woman is negative.

Thus the universe came into being through Mind—the Mind of the Maker. The earth came into existence much in the same way in which each atomic cell multiplies in itself; and worlds are still being made by the same process.

When the earth cooled and became habitable, man as man entered through the mind of the Maker. He entered into materiality in the form of flesh-man; that which carnally might die, decay, and return to dust. But the spirit in man is immortal and eternal that he may again be one with the Creator. "Know ye not that ye are the temple of God, and that the Spirit of God dwelleth in you?"

Although man has come a long way towards subduing the earth, materially and scientifically, he nevertheless persists in trying to subdue his fellow man. He has not yet fully accepted the Brotherhood of man and the Fatherhood of God. For all men are indeed brothers; there is no other real relationship.

Overcoming the monstrosities, the mixtures and the animal influences was accomplished through rebirth, surgery, and evolution towards a more divine purpose. The animal influences finally disappeared about 9000 B.C. Remnants of these pathetic creatures, with their appendages of wings, tails, feathers, claws, and hooves were later depicted accurately in Assyrian and Egyptian art. The sphinx is a notable example of one of the earlier monstrosities.

Extracts from the Cayce Readings

"When the forces of the universe came together, upon the waters was the sound of the coming of the sons of God. And the morning stars sang together. Over the face of the waters was the voice of the glory of the coming of the plane for man's indwelling. The earth in its form became a place; and afterwards able to be an abode for the creature called man." (Case # 34-L-1)

"The entity was . . . in the beginning when the first of the elements were given and the forces were first set in motion that brought about the sphere . . . called the earth plane . . . when the morning stars sang together, and the whispering winds brought the news of the coming of man's indwelling, of the spirit of the Creator; and he became a living soul. The entity came into being with that multitude."

(Case # 294–L–1)

"The entity finds itself body, mind, and soul; which answers to the Godhead—Father, Son, and Holy Ghost —in the three-dimensional world. God moved and the spirit came into activity. In the moving was brought light and then chaos. In this light came the creation of that which in the earth came to be matter; in the spheres about the earth, space and time. In patience it has evolved through those activities until there are the heavens and all the constellations, the stars, and the universe as it is known —or sought to be known—by soul-entities in the material plane.

"Then came materiality as such into the earth, through the Spirit pushing itself into matter. Spirit became individualized and then became what we recognize in one another as individual entities. Spirit which uses matter, which uses every influence in the earth's environment for the glory of the Creative Forces, partakes of—and is a part of—the Universal Consciousness.

"As the entity, the individual, then applies itself, it becomes aware through patience, through time, through space, of its relationship to the Godhead. For in itself it finds body, mind, and soul. As the Son is the builder, so is the mind the builder in the individual entity."

(Case # 3508–MS–1)

"Let it be remembered that the earth was peopled by animals before it was peopled by man! First (there was) that of a mass, about which there arose a mist; and then the rising of same, with light breaking over it as it settled itself (to be) as a companion of those (planets) in the universe; as it began its natural (or now natural) rotations, with their varied effects upon various portions of same (earth), as it slowly recedes—and is still slowly receding or gathers closer to the sun, it receives its impetus for awakening the elements that give life itself (by radiation of like elements . . . from the sun). . . . These elements have their attraction and repulsion, or . . . animosity and gathering together. This we see throughout all of the kingdom . . . whether we speak of the heavenly hosts, or of the stars, or of the planets."   (Case # 364–6)

"Man was made as man. There were—there are, as we find—only three of the creations . . . matter, force, and mind. All flesh is not one flesh, but the developing of one has always remained in the same (pattern) . . . and only has been (developed) to meet the needs of man, for whom was made all that was made. Man's evolving has only been . . . the gradual growth upward to the mind of the Maker.

"Man was made in the beginning, as the ruler over those elements which were prepared in the earth plane for his needs. When the plane became such that man was capable of being sustained by the forces and conditions . . . upon the face of the earth, man appeared. And in man there is found all that may be found without, in the whole earth plane, and other than that, the soul of man is that which makes him above the animal, the vegetable and the mineral kingdoms of the earth. Man did not descend from the monkey, but he has evolved, renewed from time to time— here a little, there a little, line upon line.

"Man is man, and God's order of creation which he represents even as (does) His Son who, as the representative of the Father, took on the form of man, the highest of the creation in the plane; and became for man the element that shows . . . the Way, the direction, the Life, the Water, the Vine to the Everlasting. . . .

"All souls were created in the beginning, and are finding their way back to whence they came."

(Case # 8337–D–276)

". . . God moved and said, *Let there be light,* and there was light. Not the light of the sun, but rather that light which—through which, in which—every soul had, and has and ever had, its being."   (Case # 5246–L–1)

"In the matter of form, as we find, there were first those projections from the animal kingdom; for the thought-bodies gradually took form; and the various combinations . . . classified themselves as gods or rulers over . . .

herds, or fowls, or fishes—in part much in the form of the present-day man . . . These took on many sizes as to stature . . . from midgets to giants, for there were giants in the earth in those days—men as tall as ten to twelve feet, and well-proportioned throughout."

(Case # 364–11)

"The earth brought forth the seed in her season, and man came in the earth plane as the lord of all in that sphere; man appearing in five places then at once. There were the five senses, the five reasons, the five spheres, the five developments, the five nations. The number of human souls in the earth plane then was 133,000,000 souls."

(Case # 5748–1, 2)

"In the beginning, as matter was impregnated with spirit of the Creative Influence, there came into being Man, in his environment that made for indwelling of the spirit with a soul that might be made one with that Creative Energy.

"That matter became impregnated with spirit arose from the very fact that spirit, separated, had erred; and only through the environment of matter or flesh might the attributes of the source of good be manifested.

"For the spirit of evil has not—did not—become manifested in matter; it has only been moved by, or upon, or through matter. . . . Just as the process of time has moved in and through matter, so there has come to man —in the finite mind—the consciousness of the indwelling of soul, spirit, body . . .

"Hence, as we find, the *mind* of man then divided for the understanding into the conscious, physical-conscious; the subconscious or unconscious-conscious; and the super- or soul-conscious of the individual entity."

(Case # 5752–3)

"For the entity came not merely by chance. For the earth is a causation world, and in the earth cause and effect are the natural law. And as each soul enters this material plane it is to meet or give such lessons or truths that others, too, may gain more knowledge of the purpose for which each soul enters . . .

"Then ye as a soul-entity in the beginning sought companionship with God; losing that companionship by choice of . . . what would satisfy or gratify merely the material desire. Thus ye, as the Master, enter again and again; coming to fulfill the law that brought that soul into being: to be one with Him."

(Case # 3645–L–1)

"Q. Do the lower forms of creation, such as animals, have souls or any life in the spirit form?

"A. All have the spirit force. Man, as he was made, carries the soul force, that which was made equal with the Creator in the beginning in relation to production in his (man's) plane of existence. Hence, the necessity for development of that soul energy . . . For in man we find both the spirit entity and the physical entity."

(Case # 900–24)

"Survival of the fittest applies in the animal kingdom, not for man. Let all read history. Which has survived—brute strength or the development towards God? Which survives—the man who studies God and seeks to emulate His forces and powers, or the man who emulates the forces of earth or flesh? This answers itself. . . ."

(Case #900–340)

"Q. Are souls perfect, as created by God in the beginning? If so, where is there any need for development?

"A. The answer to this may only be found in the evolution of life, in such a way as to be understood by the finite mind. In the First Cause or Principle, all is perfect. That portion of the whole (manifest in the creation of souls) may become a living soul and equal with the Creator. To reach that position, *when separated from Him,* it must pass through all stages of development in order that it may be one with the Creator."

(Case # 900–10)

"Q–1. The first problem concerns the reason for creation. Should this be given as God's desire to experience Himself, God's desire for companionship, God's desire for expression—or in some other way?

"A–1. God's desire for companionship and expression.

"Q–2. The second problem concerns that which is variously called evil, darkness, negation, sin. Should it be said that this condition existed as a necessary element of creation—that the soul, given free will, found itself with the power to indulge in it or lose itself in it? Or should it be said that this (evil, sin) is a condition created by the activity of the soul itself? Should it be described, in either case, as a state of consciousness, a gradual lack of awareness of self and self's relationship to God?

"A–2. It is the free will, and its losing itself in its relationship to God.

Q–3. The third problem has to do with the fall of man. Should this be described as something which was inevitable in the destiny of souls? Or something which God did not desire, but which He did not prevent once He had given free will . . . ?

"A–3. He did not prevent, once having given free will. For He made the individual entities or souls in the beginning . . . the beginnings of sin, of course, were in (the souls') seeking experiences of themselves *outside of the plan,* or the way in which God had expressed them. Thus it was the individual, see?

"Having given free will, then—and even though having foreknowledge, even though being omnipotent and omnipresent—it is only when the soul that is a portion of God *chooses,* that God knows the end thereof.

"Q–4. The fourth problem concerns man's tenancy on earth. Was it originally intended that souls remain out of earthly forms, and were the races originated as a necessity resulting from error?

"A–4. The earth and its manifestations were only the expression of God, and not necessarily as a place of tenancy for the souls of man—until man was created . . . to meet the needs of existing conditions . . .

"Q–6. The sixth problem concerns interplanetary and intersystem dwelling between earthly lives. It was given through this source that the entity . . . went to the system of Arcturus, and then returned to earth. Does this indicate a usual or an unusual step in soul evolution?

"A–6. As indicated, or has been indicated in other sources besides this, respecting this very problem—Arcturus is what may be called the centre of this universe; (the system) through which individuals pass, and at which period there comes the choice of the individual as to whether it is to return to complete (evolution) there; . . . that is, in this planetary system, our sun and its planetary system . . . or to pass on to others. This was an unusual step—and yet a usual one.

"Q–7. The seventh problem concerns implications from the sixth problem. Is it necessary to finish the solar cycle before going to other systems?

"A–7. Necessary to finish the solar cycle. . . .

"Q–9. Must the solar cycle be finished on earth, or can it be completed on another planet; or does each planet have a cycle of its own which must be finished?

"A–9. If it is begun on earth, it must be finished on the earth. The solar system of which the earth is a part is only a portion of the whole. For as indicated in the number of the planets about the earth, they are of one and the same . . . and they are relative to one another. . . .

"Q–15. Are heredity, environment and will equal factors in aiding or retarding the entity's development?

"A–15. Will is the greater factor, for it may overcome any or all of the others—provided that will is made one with the pattern, see? For no influence of heredity, environment or whatnot surpasses the will, else why would that pattern have been shown in which the individual soul—no matter how far astray it may have gone—may enter with Him into the Holy of Holies?

"Q–16. The ninth problem concerns the proper symbol or simile for the Master, the Christ. Should Jesus be described as the Soul who first went through the cycle of earthly lives to attain perfection, including perfection in the planetary lives also?

"A–16. He should be. This is as the man, see?

"Q–17. Should this be described as a voluntary mission by One who was already perfect and returned to God, having accomplished His Oneness in other planes and systems?

"A–17. Correct." (Case # 5749–14)

"The worlds were created and are still in creation—in this heterogeneous mass which is called the outer sphere;

or those portions to which man looks up in space. The mists are gathering . . . of what is this the beginning? In this same beginning, so began the earth's sphere . . ."

(Case # 900–340)

CHAPTER THREE

THE RISE AND FALL
OF ATLANTIS

Ever since Plato wrote his startling account of a sunken continent, men have debated the reality of its existence. Indeed, no historical subject has produced more controversy and been of such persistent duration. Long since lost in antiquity, here is a land and a people about which history officially knows nothing. In spite of Plato's story and some 25,000 volumes subsequently written on the subject, only the bravest of modern scholars give any credence to the Atlantean theory.

The first recorded mention of such a land is in Plato's *Timaeus,* written in the fifth century before Christ. Here the great philosopher describes a conversation between certain Egyptian priests and Solon, an Athenian statesman of the seventh century B.C. The priests represented Atlantis as a great island larger than Asia Minor and Libya combined, lying just beyond the Straits of Gibraltar. It had been a powerful kingdom 9,000 years before the birth of Solon, in 638 B.C., and its invading hordes had overrun the lands which bordered the Mediterranean.

Only Athens itself had successfully withstood the Atlantean invasions. Finally, because of the wickedness of its inhabitants, earthquakes and the sea overwhelmed Atlantis and it disappeared into the ocean. In the unfinished *Critias,* Plato adds a history of the ideal commonwealth of Atlantis —the political Utopia of another age.

Pliny, the Roman naturalist, also discusses it in his *Natural History,* a sort of encyclopaedia written in the first century A.D. Early Arabian geographers place Atlantis on their maps. Medieval writers accepted it as true history, and their beliefs were substantiated by numerous traditions of ancient islands in the eastern seas which offered various points of resemblance to Atlantis. Some of these sunken islands were marked on maps as late as the sixteenth century A.D.

There are traditions of a great flood among almost all races of ancient peoples, indicating a common origin and a widespread acceptance of the legend. In the seventeenth and eighteenth centuries the subject of Atlantis was still seriously debated, and its credibility admitted by such men as Voltaire, Montaigne, and Buffon. Francis Bacon, in his allegory, *The New Atlantis,* published in 1627, presents it as a symbolic Utopia established on scientific principles; a high cultivation of natural science and the arts.

Many attempts have since been made to rationalize the story of Atlantis, the best perhaps being *Atlantis: The Antediluvian World,* by Ignatius Donnelly. The land has variously been identified with America, the Scandinavian countries, the Canary Islands, and Palestine—but usually with the main body of it lying in the North Atlantic.

Perhaps its most prominent defender of modern times was Edward H. Thompson, archaeologist and American Consul for twenty-four years to Yucatan, Mexico. He died in 1935, still convinced that the mysterious tribe of Mayan Indians of Central America was originally from Atlantis. A few others have held to this view despite the ridicule of the conservative element of science.

Scholars have long tended to regard the whole story as invention, since no contemporary written records have been found. Little credence is given to the early accounts, the legends or the theory, although the latter does answer many otherwise unanswered questions. Plato, Pliny and Bacon are not known as writers of pointless fiction, and the story as a myth would appear to be grossly out of place in serious philosophic and historic works. Why they should now be accused of fabricating their accounts, except partially in the case of Bacon, is as regrettable as it is unrealistic and unlikely.

Geologists have discovered that the coastline of western Europe at one time extended farther in the direction of America than it does now, and that its submergence must have taken place long before history was recorded. There are known mountain ranges, ravines and ridges in the bottom of the Atlantic. Because of a broken cable running between Brest and Cape Cod, geologists found lava which proved to have hardened under atmospheric conditions—and therefore above water—less than 15,000 years ago. In Colorado an ancient dog's skull of European origin was identified as that of a species 12 to 15 million years old, suggesting a land bridge to that continent.

Archaeological findings reveal striking similarities between ancient Egyptian and Central American architecture, art and inscriptions, although the two lands are separated by thousands of miles of ocean. Atlantean migration to both areas is a plausible answer, especially since no other satisfactory solution to the problem has been put forth.

Atlantis is first mentioned in the Cayce Records in a reading given in 1923. After that, many facets of its history appear hundreds of times in readings for different persons over a period of twenty-three years. The readings not only corroborate its existence and the best that has been written on the subject, but they supply much that is new and give a detailed and comprehensive picture of the land and its peoples. More than that, and perhaps most important of all, they relate its amazing civilization to our present age in a way that is stirring, convincing, and alarming.

Interwoven in the last era of the Atlantean culture are factors that have direct and significant influences on the problems of current events at home and abroad. These are not by accident; and the numerous parallels between the two civilizations drive home the crucial importance of the decisions America now faces.

From the Cayce Records

When man entered the earth as a physical being, the land areas of the world were very different from what they are today. After the shift of the poles and the breaking up of the continents many thousands of years later, vast changes were to take place.

The polar regions were then tropical and semi-tropical. Most of the North American continent was covered with water except for the states of Utah, Nevada, Arizona and New Mexico. These were fertile plains, as was the Gobi Desert of East Asia. The Andean coastal area of South America was under water, as was most of that continent except the region of the Southern Cordilleras and Peru. The upper part of West Africa—Egypt and the Sudan—was above water, and the Nile emptied into the Atlantic Ocean.

In Europe and Asia, the regions of the Carpathian and Caucasian Mountains, Norway, Mongolia and Tibet were above sea level. Iran and the Caucasus were rich lands— the Garden of Eden.

The continents of Lemuria and Atlantis were the world's largest land areas. Lemuria, lying roughly in what was later to become the Pacific Ocean, extended from the western part of the United States to South America. The Andean coast was its tideland area, as were portions of Central America.

Atlantis, occupying largely what was later to be the North Atlantic Ocean, was the most important land area. It compared in size to Europe and Russia combined. The eastern seaboard of the United States, then mostly under water, comprised the coastal lowlands of Atlantis, which extended to the Gulf of Mexico and as far as the Mediterranean Sea. The island of Bimini off the coast of Florida was a part of the continent, as were the Bahamas in the British West Indies and Yucatan in southern Mexico.

When the perfect race appeared in Atlantis in what was known as the red race, the land was already inhabited by the monstrosities. These were the soul-entities who had taken on all sorts of strange and grotesque bodies in order to experience material existence in the earth. They had existed for hundreds of thousands of years and, as in the rest of the world, had become all shapes and sizes, from pygmies to giants twelve feet tall—with many freakish abnormalities resulting from their mixing with the animals.

At first they lived peacefully together, for the struggle of the Sons of God to *be fruitful, multiply and replenish the earth and subdue it* did not at once meet active, organized resistance. Souls born with perfect bodies continued to enter the earth in large numbers to help keep the balance and prepare for the dissensions that later were to come with the Sons of Belial—those of both races who turned away more and more from the divine will. But with this second influx of souls, some ten and a half million years ago, *even in that day did they call upon the name of the Lord.*

Swiftly they banded together in family and clan life. They ate the herbs and fruit of the now flowering earth, and for clothing wore the skins of animals (*and the Lord*

nade for them coats) to cover that portion of the body
which had already brought such destructive influences in
heir sex relations with the monstrosities. They lived in
rocks, in caves, and in trees. Motivated by the desire to
excel, to control, to dominate, households, clans and then
tribes came into existence, accelerated by the search for
companionship, protection and trade. Quickly they learned
that their well-being was dependent upon each other.

The people of Atlantis were to pass through the same
stages of development as the other four races in the various
lands, although their progress was to be more rapid. Unlike
the rest of the world, the Atlanteans as a nation were a
peaceful people at this time and more readily made use of
the laws of nature.

Stone was first utilized in implements to secure food and
protect themselves from the animals. At an early period
houses of wood, then of stone, circular in shape, were
built. First the Atlanteans were hunters; then herders and
farmers, using tools of stone and wood. Fire and natural
gas were among the first discoveries; iron and copper
quickly followed. Soon they were fabricating balloons from
the hides of elephants and other large animals and using
them for the moving of building materials. Communities
and communication slowly came into existence.

The monstrosities and the mixtures, hampered by cum-
bersome bodies and dull minds, made almost no material
progress at all, except for that passed on to them by their
masters. Physically, over the centuries, they gradually began to lose some of their animal appearance and instinct,
through intermarriage and repeated reincarnation in the
earth.

But the real problem was with the animal kingdom.
Enormous, carnivorous beasts roamed the forests of the
mountains and the jungles of the valleys. Giant fowls
hovered above the earth, feeding upon and devouring whatever was at hand. Physically inept in comparison, man had
but one superior weapon of defence: the soul-force, or
mind. By exercising the power of will and reason, he was
able to devise, to improvise, to outwit. By this means alone
was he able to survive the brute strength of the animals,
whose rule was the Survival of the Fittest.

Still relatively close to God although he had fallen into

matter, man during his first thousand years on earth was possessed of a body through which the soul expressed itself much more easily than later was to be the case. Occult powers were commonplace. The third eye, or pituitary gland, located near the centre of the forehead, was highly developed. Through this gland functioned the creative psychic abilities of the soul. Those of the perfect race thereby had knowledge of happenings in distant places and foreknowledge of events to come. They also had the power to control the monstrosities and subject them to their will. Yet man was continually drifting away from his source and submerging more and more into the material world with all its temporal interests; thus he was eventually to lose—for all practical purposes—this God-given power. These *gifts of the spirit* would remain submerged until men had again spiritualized themselves in thought and deed. Few were able to do so.

The animal kingdom became an increasing problem, and the constant threat of death made life miserable. A council of the wise men of five nations of the world, representing the five races, was called around 52,000 B.C. Representatives came from the white race in the Caucasus, the Carpathian Mountains of Central Europe, and Persia; from the yellow race in what later became the Gobi desert; the black race in the Sudan and upper West Africa; and the brown race in Lemuria. In the first meeting for united action, ways and means were planned for combating the creatures overrunning the earth in so many places. Discussions for defence centered around the use of the potent chemical forces in the elements of the earth and air. The decisions made proved to be effective, but they had unexpected and far-reaching consequences during the years ahead.

The mixtures and monstrosities were the outcasts of society. Frequently of low principle and little self-will or control, they were used for the most menial tasks. Their status in the social scale was little higher than that of domesticated animals and beasts of burden. Because of them men of the perfect race fell into two camps, bitterly opposed to each other in ideology. It was the mixing of those of pure lineage with those who had not completely overcome the animal influences that brought dissensions and the rise of strife and turmoil.

These outcasts, enslaved by those of Belial, the followers of Baal or Beelzebub—the forces of evil—were treated harshly. Through the use of occult powers, hypnosis and mental telepathy, they were under complete domination of their masters. They were bred like cattle for particular types of work and enjoyed none of the fruits of their labour and very little home life. Commonly known as *Things*— the untouchables, the automatons—they did all the work in the fields, the households, and some of the trades.

Castes and classes came into being, fostered by the Sons of Belial through greed, contempt and hatred. Bloodshed resulted from this disregard of and disrespect for the rights and freedom of others. The many were subjected to the whims of the few for their own self-aggrandizement.

The laws of heredity and environment gradually became more of an influence; appearances changed according to the purity of the strain and individual purposes—ideals and motives of activity. There were some who were almost perfect in figure and feature; and others who had monstrous combinations of human physiques and animal appendages, such as hooves, claws, feathers, wings and tails. It was these strange creatures who later were to be so mysteriously depicted in Egyptian and Assyrian inscriptions. At an early period in Egypt they were finally to disappear from the human race.

These *daughters of men* and *giants in the earth* of the Old Testament were the reason for the admonishment: *Keep the race pure.* Yet the mixtures sometimes produced divine bodies with twisted, warped souls; or repulsive bodies with souls seeking the light. It was not the body that mattered so much, but the purity of purpose, of ideals.

Through the injunction, *If you will be my people I will be your God,* an effort was made by the more spiritual-minded to draw people to the worship of the One God. Known as the Children of the Law of One, they sought to purify the race in purpose as well as in body. The tenets of those of the Law of One—One Religion, One State, One Wife, One Home, One God—had little appeal to the Sons of Belial.

The first altars were established for the sacrifice of the fruits of man's labours; the harvest of the fields and the flocks of the pastures. Religion came into being, motivated by what man felt but no longer knew to be true, although the Law of One has always been the same:

"Love ye in your daily experience. Apply in your daily activities the love that ye would have the Father show ye. In your relationships to your fellow man, do ye know the Law of One."

That was the first creed, established upon the first law of God to His children: *Hear, O Israel* (seekers), *the Lord thy God is One. Thou shalt have no other gods before Me.*

Temples were established and soon the symbols of religion—ceremonies, rituals, prayers and chants—were instituted. The sacred fires were started as the shrine of the pure and the means of cleansing and spiritualizing the mixtures who came seeking enlightenment and a more divine purpose in their lives. Religion was slowly developing as a system—a method of reminding man of his divinity. The continuity of life, or reincarnation, was recognized as an essential part of the plan of evolution for the soul. Karma, the law of cause and effect in action, or *As ye sow, so shall ye reap*, was fundamental.

Thus the breach between those of the Law of One and those of Belial slowly took form, a breach that later was to widen into a gulf. The carnal, materialistic way of life of the followers of Belial was attractive even to many of the Children of the Law of One, and numbers of them succumbed to the temptations. With the emphasis on the value of temporal things and the de-emphasis on the spiritual, idol worship crept into the religious scene.

The first of the series of three continental catastrophes occurred about 50,700 B.C., many thousands of years before the final drowning. It came as a material result of the use of chemicals and high explosives in the plan to annihilate the wild beasts. The real reason was the low state into which man had fallen.

Huge and numerous gas pockets were blown open in the lairs of the animals, precipitating volcanic eruptions and earthquakes in the still slowly cooling earth. The magnitude of the disturbances caused the axis of the world to shift, bringing the poles to their present position and producing the last of the great Ice Ages.

Lemuria was the first to be affected, losing much of its territory as it began to sink into the Pacific. In Atlantis the area of the Sargasso Sea, off the west coast of Cuba, was the first to go under water. The rest of the continent was broken up into several large islands with many canals, ravines, gulfs, bays and streams. The temperate climate rapidly changed to a more torrid one.

With the upheavals, the initial migrations from Atlantis took place in small numbers to the east and west. The earliest settlements were in the region of the Pyrenees Mountains in France and Spain; then later in Central and South America. The movement of the Lemurians was primarily to South America. The land of Og, along the Pacific coastal area of what was later to be southern Peru, was occupied. This was the beginning of that mysterious tribe of Indians known as the Incas.

From this time on, although material civilization rose to great heights, there was growing unrest among the Atlantean people. In a land of plenty, strife rather than peace became the rule. The altars came to be used for human sacrifice by those turning away from the original concept of the One God. Sun worship became prevalent. Only the dedicated, inner core of the Children of the Law of One remained firm.

Low standards of morality, sex indulgence and perversion became rampant. Poverty and hunger were widespread among the peasantry and working classes. There was a deteriorating of the physical and spiritual bodies, just as there was a wasting away of the mountains and valleys into the seas. In spite of material advancements and many scientific achievements, inner decay was to bring dispersion and finally annihilation to a proud, wicked, adulterous people.

The second important land change came long after the first, around 28,000 B.C., and resulted in the submergence of many large islands. The Bible gives an account of it in the story of Noah and the Flood.

After the deluge, which was preceded by volcanic eruptions and electrical storms, the principal land areas left in this part of the world were the islands of *Poseidia* in the North (West Indies area), *Aryaz* in the central Atlantic and *Og* (Peru) in the West. There were large movements of the people to these lands as well as to other parts of the earth.

Lemuria vanished into the Pacific Ocean. Some of its inhabitants fled to the safety lands of lower California, Arizona and New Mexico, where they established the Brotherhood of Mu in the land of "Mayra".

For the Atlanteans it was the end of an era, and the beginning of a new one unsurpassed in many ways.

After the days of the Flood, a period of rebuilding began in Atlantis. The Atlantean scientific turn of mind combined with their energy and aggressiveness made possible great strides forward in mechanics, chemistry, physics and psychology; for in many ways the Atlanteans were a superior people. In certain fields they were more learned than any civilization since.

When electricity was discovered after the first upheaval, it paved the way for remarkable developments in the field of electronics and electrical devices. Atomic power, from uranium, came to be understood and used in transportation and the movement of heavy objects. It was also abused, for selfish purposes. The Atlanteans had more efficient systems of heating and lighting; and communications with other lands were well established. Light rays of many kinds, such as laser beams, were discovered and controlled, including the death ray. Liquid air was manufactured, also compressed air and rubber. Metal alloys of brass, aluminum and uranium, unknown to us, were used in the construction of air and water craft, including the submarine. The telephone and the elevator were in common use; radio and television were highly developed, as was the amplification of light rays in telescopic observation and photographing at long distances. Many types of bodily adornment came to be fabricated. Soldiering and law enforcement became a part of the political scene.

But the most notable scientific accomplishment of the Atlanteans was the harnessing of the sun's energy. Developed originally as a means of spiritual communication between the finite and the infinite, the huge reflective crystals were first known as the *Tuaoi* Stone. Later, as its use was improved upon over the centuries, it expanded to become a generator of power or energy, radiating across the land without wires. Then it became known as the *Firestone*, or the *Great Crystals*.

Set in the Temple of the Sun in Poseidia, the Firestone was the central power station of the country. Basically, it was a large cylindrical glass or stone of many facets, capped with a mechanism at one end. It was suspended in the centre of the building and insulated with a non-conductive material akin to asbestos but resembling bakelite. Above the stone was a dome which could be rolled back for exposure to the sun.

The concentration and magnification of the sun's rays through the many prisms was of tremendous intensity. So powerful was it that it could be regenerated and transmitted throughout the land in invisible beams similar to radio waves. Its energy was used to power ships at sea, aircraft and even pleasure vehicles. This was done by remote control through induction methods to the apparatus in the craft. Cities and towns received their power from the same source.

The human body could even be rejuvenated through the moderate application of the rays from the crystals, and man often rejuvenated himself. Yet by mis-application, the Firestone could be and was turned to destructive uses as well as the means for torture and punishment. Tuned too high—not intentionally—it contributed to the cause of the second catastrophe. The rays combined with other electrical forces to start many fires deep within the earth, and volcanic eruptions were precipitated from nature's powerful storehouse of energy.

Beautiful stone cities that glistened in the sunlight were scattered across the land. Among them were *Amaki, Achaei* and *Poseidia;* the latter being the most important city of the day. It was located on the last of the great islands designated by the same name. Here on the *Bay of Parfa* was one of the best and busiest seaports of the world.

Water was supplied to the buildings of the city and the many pools and lagoons by viaducts built to nearby mountain streams. So huge and numerous were these conduits that they gave the appearance of a walled city. Water sports were highly popular. The buildings were constructed in tiers with gleaming, polished stones and intricate mosaics of superior craftsmanship.

In the centre of the city was the temple, around which much of the life of the Children of the Law of One revolved. Supported by huge, semi-circular columns of onyx, topaz and beryl inlaid with amethyst and other colourful stones, the elaborate temple reflected the rays of the sun from a variety of beautiful angles.

Inside, the sacred fires of the altars burned constantly in the inner chamber. These mysterious flames produced rays —the knowledge of which was so soon to be lost—that were used in the treatments given the Mixtures for the removal of unwanted appendages. There was a large outer court which served as an assembly hall, and inner rooms for the prophets and the many priests, priestesses and attendants of the temple. The large priesthood was made up of the most learned men and women of the day, and some of them acted in the capacity of judges as well as spiritual and vocational instructors.

The Atlanteans, and especially the Poseidians, studied the creative energies of the universe and penetrated the essence of nature's storehouse; the vibrations of plants, jewels and metals—the latter including their vibratory effect on the psychic and intuitive nature of man. Agriculture was highly advanced, as were astronomy and astrology. The Atlanteans calculated the meaning of numbers, the stars and the elements; and even knew the activity and effect of the morning dew. They learned how to neutralize the pull of gravity. They were aware of the mysteries of the origin of man and the five races, and they had a full understanding of the laws of metaphysics—of spiritual and scientific truths which are essentially the same.

It was this wealth of knowledge possessed by those of the Law of One that was sought and misapplied by those of Belial, the materialists who rejected not only the ideas of the worshippers of the One God but also their precautions and warnings. There were some of the Law of One who listened to the arguments and the temptations offered by those of Belial and yielded, becoming collaborators with them in the desire to use for pleasure and destructive purposes the creative energies and laws of the universe.

This misapplication was known as the "Nightside" of the law, or of life. Many religious temples were degraded to temples of sin as spiritual laws were applied to the satisfaction of the physical appetites. The misuse of psychic powers brought strife in many quarters. There was contention over the use of explosives, gases and liquid air for selfish purposes. Conflicts arose over special privileges and who were to be the leaders as well as which was to be the ruling party of the land. The slave, peasantry and working class were not only selfishly oppressed and abused, but heavily taxed as well. Party lines were thus sharply drawn between the two groups. Although those of the One God were ostensibly in power, large inroads in their authority and control were made by the opposition, the self-seeking groups. Civil war erupted.

The form of government was a monarchy in a semi-socialist state. The king was aided in his rule by an inner council. In this there were evil elements; and deceit, intrigue and conspiracy were within the king's own household. Society was divided generally into three classes: the ruling class—those of both groups in positions of power and authority, including the high priesthood; the middle or teaching class—instructors and overseers; and the peasantry or labouring class, including the mixtures. There was also a line of royalty, and princes and princesses who loved the pomp and splendour about the king's court. The Children of the Law of One lived communally.

The growth of disturbing factors within, the magnification of personal desires and embitterments, made the final destruction of Atlantis all the more certain. Advanced understanding of spiritual and natural laws and their misapplication made that destruction all the more terrible. Those of the One God realized, through the clairvoyant powers of the fast-declining pituitary gland, that the impending final breakup of the Poseidian-Atlantean lands was now at hand. They sought ways of warning and uniting the people in order to prevent it, if possible, so that they might still carry out the injunction, *Subdue the earth*, rather than —as those of Belial would have it—*subdue one another*.

They endeavoured to gather all the knowledge of the various nations of the world concerning the approaching disaster, and a meeting was called with this in view. Envoys from many lands came to Atlantis to pool their wisdom in a last attempt to avert the calamity, but the meeting and the evangelistic campaign resulting from it were to no avail.

Reconciled to the inevitable national cataclysm, the Children of the Law of One made other plans; the search for suitable lands to colonize. Many expeditions went out for this purpose. The Children of the Law of One also supplied leadership in the actual movements via land, air and water to the safety lands in Egypt, Honduras, Yucatan and other areas. Of special interest to them was the preservation of their religious tenets and records, and these were taken with them.

By 10,700 B.C., the country had reached the depths of moral and spiritual life—not in knowledge but in practice. Human sacrifice and sun worshipping were prevalent, as were adultery and corruption. The mixtures were used and abused.

The forces of nature were misused. The sun crystals were cruelly adapted as a means of coercion, torture and punishment; and they became known among the common people as the "Terrible Crystals". A new low in morality and human dignity had been reached. Violence and rebellion spread across the land.

Then came the final catastrophe.

Gigantic land upheavals shook the foundations of the earth. Great islands crumbled into the sea and were inundated. Only scattered mountain peaks remained to mark the sunken graves. Some people escaped; a few stayed behind heroically to aid others in the exodus to other lands. The majority were lost. By 9500 B.C., Atlantis as a nation had vanished from the face of the earth.

The Atlantean culture, however, did not entirely pass away. Although there were comparatively high civilizations in China, India and the Pyrenees, Atlantean influence was felt in many places at different times, just as their aggressive and progressive nature is now and will continue to be felt through reincarnation in the earth.

The cycle of history often repeats itself, and the spirit of Atlantis has arisen once more, as will portions of the land itself. When changes that are to come about do take place, the island of Poseidia will be among the first high points to appear above sea level; new land will emerge off the east coast of the United States. This can be expected in 1968 or 1969.

The Bahama Islands are remnants of the peaks of Poseidia, a part of the once great continent before its breaking up into islands after the second disaster. Near the islands of Bimini, fifty miles off the coast of Miami, Florida, there are buried under ages of sea slime the remains of an old Atlantean temple. It will one day be recovered.

In the Pyrenees and Morocco are the ruins of early settlements still to be uncovered. In Honduras, Guatemala and Yucatan, Mexico, the fleeing Atlanteans became known as the Mayas. In North America they settled in New Mexico, Arizona, Nevada, Colorado and as far east as Mississippi and Ohio, where they came to be known as the Mound Builders. The Iroquois Indians are direct descendants, and traces of Atlantean religious beliefs may be found among other Indian tribes.

In Egypt, Atlantean influence was felt in the building of the pyramids. There are to be found in Egypt, Bimini and Yucatan duplicate reports of Atlantean history. The records are identical and they will clarify some of the Old Testament accounts. Included in the records are the plans for construction of the Great Crystals. Some of these remains have already been unknowingly recovered by unsuspecting archaeologists in the pyramids of Yucatan.

While the earliest recorded date in the Cayce readings is ten and a half million years ago—the second influx of souls of the perfect race—civilizations rose and fell many times during the great Atlantean period from 200,000 to 10,700 B.C. Between the first and the last destructions was a span of years many times the length of the Christian era to date. The type of culture carried into the Pyrenees and America when the first catastrophe occurred differed from that taken to Central America and Morocco with the second exodus; and to Egypt and Yucatan, Mexico, with the third and final disaster. Nor could the whole civilization in its entirety be transplanted at any time. A division of tongues took place when the continent was broken up into islands, although the rest of the world still spoke the one language. This further complicated the Atlantean effect on the various civilizations to which the people migrated.

Thus man evolves materially and sometimes spiritually, but almost never in a straight line, although generally the trend has always been upward. Here he is a little better; there a little worse; fluctuating like a cork in the sea. Souls rose to great heights; often they fell to low depths, taking others with them. But always there have been the few who were searching for the answer to the mystery of whence they came and whither they are going, and why. The higher way to a more noble and Godly life still evades man, yet it is at his finger tips.

The present age is a replica in many ways of ancient Atlantis at its height, and our technology can therefore be better understood in the light of Atlantean accomplishments. Atlanteans are now reincarnating in the earth in large numbers, and as the cycle of mankind progresses through the laws of karma—action and reaction—men are faced once again with a world of their own making. Our high civilization presents the first opportunity, under similar circumstances, not only to recompense for the many evils committed but to choose once more between the use of nature's forces for constructive or destructive purposes.

The Cayce Records say: "As indicated here, this entity is an Atlantean. Hence it is manifesting in the earth at this period when many Atlanteans have entered. For of this ye may be very sure: no leader in any country or clime—whether friend or foe of what the entity believes—is other than an Atlantean.

"As we have indicated, the Atlanteans had reached such an advancement; and had been entrusted with divine activities in the earth. But—as did also this entity—they forgot from Whom and in Whom all live and have their being. Thus they brought about within themselves that which destroyed the body, but not the soul.

"Then this is the purpose of the entity in the earth: to be a channel of blessing to someone *today—now*. That is, to be a living example of that which He gave: 'Come unto me, all that are weak and heavy laden; take my cross upon you and *learn of me*.' These are thy purposes in the earth. And these thou wilt manifest beautifully—or again make a miserable failure, as thou didst in Atlantis and as many another soul is doing in this particular era."

(Case # 2794–L–I)

We are at the threshold of the testing period. What we do now will decide the fate of mankind for ages to come.

Extracts from the Cayce Readings

"From time to time in the information obtained for some individuals in their life readings, has come (the information) that they, as an entity or individual, occupied some particular place or performed some activity in that continent; or emigrated from the continent to some other portion of the earth's surface at the time and began another particular development. These must have been a busy folk, for with their advent into other climes they began to make many changes in that sphere in which they entered.

"Be it true that there is the fact of reincarnation, and that souls that once occupied such an environ are entering the earth's sphere . . . in the present; is it any wonder that if they made such alterations in the affairs of the earth in their day as to bring destruction upon themselves, if they are entering now they might make many changes in the affairs of peoples and individuals? Are they, then, being born into the world? If so, what were the environs—and what will those environs mean in the material world today?"

(Case # 364–I)

"As an Atlantean during those periods when questions arose . . . as to the acknowledgement of the castes in the land, where the untouchables were considered as but dogs among the higher castes. The entity was in that position (where it attempted) to gain for the untouchables an approach for their own self-development. In the present, as a result of this experience, the entity has knowledge or ability in things pertaining to the working of metals and buildings . . . and the democratic feeling."

(Case # 333–L–I)

". . . the entity was a teacher among the people of that period and among those destroyed in the overflow of the land—and again will the entity be in the earth's sphere when a change comes about. In the name of Isshuta, the entity lost through this experience through fear created in self by misleading others when the truth was known. In the present, that fear is innate."   (Case # 105–L–I)

"The days upon the earth were then counted in tens and fifties and hundreds, besides the days or weeks or years as in the present . . . Or, in that experience, to live to five, six, or seven hundred years was not more than to live to the age of fifty, sixty or seventy years in the present."

(Case # 1968–L–2)

". . . As indicated, the entity was associated with those who dealt with mechancal appliances and their application during the experience. And as we find, it was a period when there was much that has not even been thought of yet in the present experience.

"About the firestone . . . the entity's activities then made such applications as dealt both with the constructive as well as destructive forces in that period. It would be well that there be given something of a description of this so that it may be understood better by the entity in the present . . .

"In the centre of a building which would today be said to be lined with non-conductive metals or non-conductive stone—something akin to asbestos, with . . . other non-conductors such as are now being manufactured in England under a name which is well known to many of those who deal in such things.

"The building above the stone was oval, or a dome wherein there could be . . . a portion for rolling back, so that the activity of the stone was received from the sun's rays or from the stars—the concentration of energies that emanate from bodies that are on fire themselves, along with the elements that are found and not found in the earth's atmosphere.

"The concentration through the prisms or glass (as would be called in the present) was in such manner that it acted upon the instruments which were connected with the various modes of travel; through induction methods which made much the character of control as would in the present day be remote control through radio vibrations or directions; through the kind of force impelled from the stone acting upon the motivating forces in the crafts themselves.

"There was preparation so that when the dome was rolled back there might be little or no hindrance in this direct application to various crafts that were to be impelled through space—whether within the radius of visioning of the one eye, as might be termed, or whether directed under water or under other elements, or through other elements.

"The preparation of this stone was solely in the hands of the initiates at the time; and the entity was among those who directed the influences of the radiation which arose, in the form of rays that were invisible to the eye but acted upon the stones themselves as set in the motivating forces —whether the aircraft . . . were lifted by the gases in the period; or whether for guiding the more-of-pleasure vehicles that might pass along close to the earth; or what would be termed the crafts on the water or under the water.

"These, then, were impelled by the concentration of rays from the stone which was centred in the middle of the power station, or power house (as would be the term in the present).

"In the active forces of these, the entity brought destructive forces by setting up—in various portions of the land —the kind that was to act in producing powers for the various forms of the people's activities in the cities, the towns and the countries surrounding same. These, not intentionally, were *tuned too high;* and brought the second period of destructive forces to the peoples in the land— and broke up the land into those isles which later became the periods when further destructive forces were brought into the land.

"Through the same form of fire, the bodies of individuals were regenerated: by burning—through application of rays from the stone—the influence that brought destructive forces to an animal organism. Hence the body often rejuvenated itself; and it remained in that land until the eventual destruction, joining with the peoples who made for the breaking-up of the land—or joining with Belial, at the final destruction of the land. In this, the entity lost. At first it was not the intention nor desire for destructive forces. Later it was for ascension of power itself.

"As for description of the manner of construction of the stone: we find it was a large cylindrical glass (as would be termed today); cut with facets in such manner that the capstone on top of it made for centralizing the power or force that concentrated between the end of the cylinder and the capstone itself.

"As indicated, the records as to ways of constructing same are in three places in the earth, as it stands today: in the sunken portions of Atlantis, or Poseidia, where a portion of the temples may yet be discovered under the slime of ages of sea water—near what is known as Bimini, off the coast of Florida. And (secondly) in the temple records that were in Egypt, where the entity acted later in cooperation with others towards preserving the records that came from the land where these had been kept. Also (thirdly) the records that were carried to what is now Yucatan, in America, where these stones (which they know so little about) are now—during the last few months—being uncovered."   (Case # 440–5)

". . . in that known as the Atlantean land, during the periods when there were turmoil and strife, from the rejections by many of the laws and tenets of One; when the upheavals began, making for egress from that Poseidian land. The entity dwelt among those where there was storage of the motivative forces in nature, from the great crystals that so condensed the lights, the forms, the activities as to guide the ships upon the bosom of the sea, and in the air; and in many of those conveniences (now known) for man: as in transmission of body, transmission of voice, recording of those activities in what is soon to become a practical thing —in the creating of vibrations such as to make for television, as termed in the present."   (Case # 813–L–I)

". . . in the Atlantean land during those particular periods when there was the exodus from Atlantis owing to foretelling . . . of those activities which were bringing about destructive forces. There we find the entity was among those who were not only in what is now known as the Yucatan land, but also the Pyrenees and the Egyptian land.

"For the manners of transportation, the ways of communications through the airships of that period were such as Ezekiel described in a much later date."

(Case # 1859–L–I)

". . . in the Atlantean land during those experiences when there was an egress of the peoples, before the periods of the final destruction. The entity was among those who helped in coordinating (arrangements) with those of the various lands to which they were to journey.

"Then the entity was not only something of judge and jury—as would be termed today—but was one entrusted with the mission of seeking out lands which would give the proper surroundings, environs and activities for the peoples. And the entity came into that land now known as Central American land, where the people built many of the temples that are being uncovered today.

"As the entity reads or hears of these, they become of particular interest, for these are a portion of the entity's experience. The entity may answer much that has been questioned in the minds of those who have sought to know *why* there are no remains of the settlements or peoples that left the land without showing any *burial grounds*. For the entity was one who began the custom of cremating; and the ashes of much of this may be found in one of those temples which was prepared for this purpose."

(Case # 914–L–I)

". . . in the Atlantean land during the periods when there were beginnings of the exodus owing to the destructive forces that had been begun by the sons of Belial.

"The entity was among the princes of the land who made for separating the influences wherein might be established the journeyings to other lands, along with the keeping of records, and . . . permanent establishment of activities that have become a part of what ye call civilization in the present time.

"Hence . . . establishments in the Yucatan, in the Luzon, in what became the Inca, in the North American

land, and in what later became the land of the Mound
Builders in Ohio; also the establishment of activities in
the upper portion of what is now the eastern portion of
the land.

"The entity then was one skilled not only in aircraft and
watercraft—as an aviator and navigator; but also made
great strides in keeping in touch with other lands, through
the forces of nature. . . . Hence those things of nature
that pertain to *communications* become a part of the entity's experience. The imagination . . . in tales of travels
. . . that have to do with strange lands, strange people
and customs, become a part of the innate forces."

(Case # 1215–L–I)

"The entity was among those who searched more than
one land to which there might be sent those who were to
be saved. Hence there was knowledge of the Yucatan land,
and the settlings in the Pyrenees, as well as (knowledge of)
activities in the Egyptian land.

"In the present, then, innately as well as manifestly, we
find that those peoples become of interest to the entity;
their customs and the motivating influences in their lives.

"We find that the entity was a sojourner in Poseidia in
the earlier portion of that experience; but when determining factors arose from the disputes between the children of
the Law of One and the sons of Belial, the entity was
among those who journeyed to the Egyptian land during
the period of reconstruction.

"Hence we find abilities arising from those combinations
of purposes, along the lines of activities in which greater
satisfaction, greater development may come for the entity."

(Case # 1908–L–I)

"Before that, the entity was in the Atlantean land when
there were turmoils, just before the second breaking-up
of the land; when there were those discussions and turmoils between the sons of Belial and the children of the
Law of One.

"The entity joined with those who sought to attempt to
use the material advantages of the sons of Belial, but to
keep the principles of the children of the Law of One. Thus
cross-purposes ensued between the mental and the ma-

terial ideals of the entity. But the Lord thy God is one, and not a house divided against itself."

(Case # 3102–L–I)

". . . in the Atlantean land during the periods when there was the breaking up of the land and there had been the edict that the land must be changed.

"The entity was among those who set sail for the Egyptian land but entered into the Pyrenees, and what is now the Portuguese, French and Spanish lands. *And there still may be seen in the chalk cliff there in Calais* the marks made by the entity's followers, as attempts were made . . . to create a temple activity for the followers of the Law of One.

". . . The entity lost and gained. . . . Gained when there was establishing of associations with those who had built up the Egyptian land. And as will be seen from those things . . . yet to be found about Alexandria; the entity may be said to have been the first to begin the establishment of the library of knowledge in Alexandria, ten thousand three hundred years before the Prince of Peace entered Egypt for His first initiation there. For read ye: 'He was crucified also in Egypt.' "

(Case # 315–L–I)

CHAPTER FOUR

THE PYRAMID BUILDERS

Of all the mysteries in the earth, the Great Pyramid of Egypt stands foremost in one respect: More has been written about it than any other man-made structure. As one of the Seven Wonders of the world, it has long been the object of spurious speculation and debate regarding its age, purpose, and manner of erection. Yet, the whole of Egypt, in fact, *is* a rich and fascinating field for scholarly research, for here lie some of man's most baffling riddles.

The earliest known date in world history is that of the adoption of the Egyptian calendar, in 4241 B.C. A widely accepted system divides the history of the land into thirty dynasties—from 3400 to 332 B.C. Almost nothing is known of the times prior to these, although none of these dates is fixed beyond doubt. The Great Pyramid of Gizeh is generally believed to have been constructed about 2900 B.C.

It is located ten miles west of the old and historic city of Cairo, at Latitude 29° 58′ 51″ North; Longitude 31° 09′ East (Greenwich). It is thought to be a burial tomb for King Khufu, or Cheops, although no remains were found there. The huge pyramid covers a little over thirteen acres and measures 760 feet at each baseline and 481 feet in height.

The Great Pyramid is the only one that has a square base and that is constructed entirely of stone, huge blocks of yellow limestone weighing as much as 54 tons each. The precision of its erection is so exact that it may be compared to the work of a lens grinder on a scale of acres. The joints are hardly discernible, and how the heavy stones were raised and fitted into place has long puzzled the engineering world. Originally it was covered with thick slabs of fine, white limestone, but this was later stripped off, as was the capstone or apex.

In geometric form, the Great Pyramid is what is called a true pyramid. Its base is a perfect square; each of its four sides is a perfect equilateral triangle which slants evenly inward and upward from the base, in the proportion of 10 to 9, until the four meet at an apex situated squarely perpendicularly over the centre of the base, where the two base-diagonals intersect.

The bearings of the base with respect to true east and west, north and south show an error of only 5 seconds—far and away the most accurately orientated building known to engineering science.

The Great Sphinx is the stone figure of a lion body with a human head. It is 189 feet long and is cut out of a single block of stone. Known as *Hu* in Egypt, it represents the god Horus, and antedates the Great Pyramid by many years. Other sphinxes, smaller in size, depict the upper part of a ram or falcon, and many inscriptions present human bodies with animal appendages of horns, hooves, claws, tails and feathers.

Egypt is not alone in having mysterious sphinxes and pyramids. In Assyria there are sphinxes distinguished by having wings, and there are also Persian and Greek sphinxes miniature in size. In Yucatan, Mexico, the remains of the Mayan culture reveal sphinxes and pyramids strikingly similar to their Egyptian counterparts but smaller in size. The power and riches required to build such structures are evident, and they indicate high civilisations of considerable wealth as well as a common source.

In early Egypt astronomy was an important science, but little has been discovered about their religion. Indeed, their beliefs appear to have been deliberately kept secret. Sun worship apparently was prevalent. The name *Re* or *Ra* was attached to the sun god, the chief of all gods. He may have come from the Caucasus. *Isis*, the prototype of all goddesses, was the nature goddess. Her worship as a deity presumably began about 1700 B.C. The "Two Lands" of Upper and Lower Egypt appear to have been united by Ra. Church and state clearly were interrelated with each other.

So little is known of ancient Egypt, in spite of the wealth of evidence, that it remains clouded in speculation and "mythology". In fact, much that has been discovered is not altogether understood, and it is on these very points that the Edgar Cayce readings cast a new light. Out of these readings emerges a concept of this prehistoric period that is as convincing as it is illuminating.

They give a much earlier date—around 10,000 B.C.—for the construction of the Great Pyramid and Sphinx; and a significance is attached to both which relates them to man's spiritual evolution in the earth. The marked cultural similarities of Egypt and Yucatan are explained by the migrations of peoples to both lands from the sunken continent of Atlantis.

The line drawings of human beings with animal appendages are explained realistically; Isis comes to life; and the ancient manuscript, *The Book of the Dead,* takes on new meaning.

This, then, is the story of Egypt's first pyramid builders, according to the Cayce readings, without the introduction of outside sources or opinionated material.

From the Cayce Records

For nearly a quarter of a million years Egypt was under water except for the regions of the Sahara and the upper Nile Valley. After other dry land appeared, it was still many centuries before much of the country was habitable. The first tribal rule, of the black race, was established in the fertile area of the upper Nile, near what later became known as the Valley of the Tombs. The people lived in tents and caves and made early use of beasts of burden. Although comparatively free from the invasions of the wild animals which were causing so much havoc in other parts of the earth, it was a weak nation beset with many inner stresses and strains.

Peace came during the second rule, that of King *Raai,* a wise and spiritual-minded man who had a broad understanding of universal laws. An effort was made to bring to the masses of the people a knowledge of the divine spark dwelling in them. In his twenty-eighth year, this King called a meeting of the world's leaders. Forty-four priests, seers and astrologers met to discuss subjects which would hasten man's development and his ability to cope with physical conditions, including the problem of the beasts in other lands. These leaders gathered in tents and caves, and the theme of the council was the *spirit forces in man that make him supreme in the earth*. King Raai was the first to make it understood that this power in relatively weak man comes from a Higher Source.

The approach was through the evidence of the force of the sun's rays, the influence of the moon, and the waters bringing forth life. Formulated here was the first law of self-preservation attributed to divine power—man's first recognition of an intellect, a power greater than his own.

This was the beginning of the study of the spiritual nature of man: the relation of man to man and man to the whole; the divisions of the mind—the conscious, subconscious and superconscious; the divisions of the solar systems and the various planes of existence through which man must pass for his development. Such tenets covered many phases of man's tenure in the earth, as symbolized by the sun, the moon, the stars and the elements. The inscribing of these spiritual laws on tablets of stone and slate became the first bible. This was the beginning of *The Book of the Dead*, as it later became known, and it was not formulated as a funeral ritual although it was interpreted as such.

The second rule in Egypt covered 199 years, and King Raai was afterwards worshipped as the representative of God made manifest in the earth. He did not provide a king the whole of his lifetime, however, because his country was invaded.

About this time, 11,016 years before the coming of the Christ or 300 years before the last of the land eruptions in Atlantis, there lived in the land of Arart (the region of the Caucasian Mountains of Eastern Europe) a large group of people of the white race. The ruler, named *Arart,* was influenced by the prophecy of a godly young priest called *Ra-Ta.*

At the age of twenty-one, Ra-Ta predicted that the people of the tribe of *Zu* who had migrated from Arabia, would march on Egypt and rejuvenate it for the betterment of both races. Egypt would then become the leading nation of the day, he prophesied. Arart, the King, at the urging of Ra-Ta became convinced of the success of such a venture and prepared for the long journey to Egypt. The expedition, led by Arart and guided by Ra-Ta, was destined to set up the first dynasty and play an important part in the history of the nation.

King Raai had become so engrossed in his metaphysical studies that he failed to heed the warnings of his advisors that he must defend the country against the threatened invasion from the north. Almost without opposition, Arart swept down upon the kingdom and conquered it. Raai surrendered immediately rather than be a party to the shedding of his people's blood, an action that brought quick condemnation from many quarters in Egypt. It was, however, a blessing in disguise. Although Raai gained spiritually for his attitude, the real importance of his life's work lay in the years ahead when it was to become the basis for a new religious concept and incorporated in the *Book of the Dead*.

At first there was a great deal of strife and contention between the conquerors and the conquered. The leader of opposition to the conquerors was not Raai but a native scribe of considerable influence and following. He was sufficiently strong to incite rebellion over a tax law just as the new king was about to bring order out of the confusion. Arart, aware of being a foreign conqueror and therefore personally unpopular with the Egyptians, made a bold and clever political manoeuvre. He abdicated the throne in favour of his young son, *Araaraat;* and at the same time he appointed the belligerent native scribe to high office and membership in the official family, with the title of Aarat. This immediately silenced the enemy and gained the support of the Egyptian people.

Another factor which helped to ease the unsettled internal situation was the attraction of the deposed King Raai to one of the beautiful maiden daughters of the invaders, who eventually became his companion. She became renowned for her beauty and virtue, and so beloved by both peoples that upon her death she was revered as a goddess. Her name was *Isai*.

At the youthful age of sixteen, in the city of Luz, the young King Araaraat undertook the formidable task of directing the destiny of a nation made up of many peoples —for there were already emigrants from India, Mongolia and Atlantis, in addition to the native Egyptians.

During the eighty-eight years of his rule there were

periods of strife as well as peace, both within and without the land. King Araaraat was aided in government affairs by an inner council of twelve advisers and an official cabinet consisting of heads of various departments: labour, economics, commerce, chemistry, construction, education, history, and the arts—especially music. These leaders were wisely chosen from among the Egyptians, the Atlanteans and the white conquerors from the north.

With the gradual sinking of the once powerful continent of Atlantis into the ocean, Atlantean refugees were by now coming to the country in large numbers. They brought with them their slaves and mixtures, their religion, and some of their advanced science. At one time during the process of solidifying the government, Arart was compelled to come out of retirement to put down an attempt by certain ambitious Atlanteans to overthrow the rule of his son. They sought to take advantage of the unsettled political situation and establish themselves in power. This ambition was short-lived, however, due to Arart's quick action. With the coming of peace within, and the amicable settling of differences of opinion, great strides forward were made in many directions. The Egyptian scribe, *Aarat,* at the age of thirty-two, became a leader in the coalition government and worked closely with young King Araaraat for the good of all factions. He helped to formulate and execute both civil and religious laws. He was a methodical recorder, and many of his inscriptions may still be found in a tomb near the Sphinx, which was in part constructed during his lifetime.

After much opposition, Ra-Ta, the prophet of the invaders, was proclaimed High Priest of Egypt. He was to direct the spiritual studies and metaphysical research of the country for many years. Ra-Ta had definite ideas about the nature of man and his relation to the whole. He was interested in both the physical and spiritual evolution of man; specifically, the continuity of life, or the immortality of the soul not only from physical birth but from the very beginning; the law of karma, or cause and effect on the spiritual level; and the concurrent indwelling of souls in other planes for their further evolution, mental in character. Ra-Ta taught that with proper schooling it was within the realm of possibility to communicate with these souls.

But most important and revolutionary, he taught the law of the One God—"The Lord thy God is One"—as against the worship of the sun, which up to that time had been the religion of the Egyptians.

The natives at first were not inclined toward such teachings. Because of the wealth of the land and the easy material life they led, they were more interested in present amenities as physical entities than in any future incarnations in the earth or spiritual life in the cosmic planes.

Up to this period the social order of the Egyptian nation was unlike that of the more advanced Atlanteans. Although there were clans and tribes, there were no family households. By state law, all the women of a tribe were housed at night in a separate temple of their own, with the males residing outside. Even the King's own residence was no exception to this rule; he lived with his servants and certain of his advisers, but no queen nor companion dwelt with him. The relations for the propagation of the race, while considered sacred, were consummated in special temples set aside for this purpose. These buildings were three or four tiers high and contained many chambers, seven by nine feet in size. There was also a large hall for dancing and recreation. Furnishings consisted of handmade rugs, blankets and couches.

Matings were not by the personal choice of the participants but at the decree of the King, with the good of the race in view. Children born in the Temple of the Hall of Birth were taken from their mothers at the age of three months and reared for the state by specially trained groups, in buildings dedicated to this purpose.

The High Priest Ra-Ta viewed this whole procedure with distaste. In his many travels to other lands—Atlantis in particular—he noted the benefits of family ties. He perceived the moral values of family life for the people—the consecration of individual lives one to another for a purpose, and the responsibilities attached to such consecration.

Upon return from one of his Atlantean trips, Ra-Ta decreed as a first step in working towards the family unit, that henceforth all men were to be restricted to one companion. For himself he chose the mother of his children, the mate who had come with him from the north. The ruling proved to be a popular one, even though the choice of mate and care of the offspring were still under the control of the government. It was, nevertheless, one of the great strides forward in the social life of Egypt.

Over the years, Ra-Ta gained in popularity and influence, although he provoked dislike among many ambitious Egyptians by urging the King to select for high office only those natives who could be proved honest, competent and loyal. This policy met opposition from the well-to-do and prominent, who sought powerful positions so that they could control and exploit the people for their own benefit. Although the type of government was a monarchy, as eventually established it was not unlike representative democracy in principle if not in method.

When Ra-Ta's archaeological research and findings began to uncover remains showing there had been an earlier civilization in Egypt, the natives gradually began to listen to his ideas concerning the Oneness of All and the One God for all.

Ra-Ta's studies in metaphysics convinced him that through the knowledge of the workings of divine law, man's process of evolution could be speeded up. He believed it possible to achieve a perfect race, mentally and physically, in less time than was required by the natural processes of birth and rebirth. His great hope was to produce perfect bodies, eventually; and it was in the implementation of these theories that Ra-Ta made his most important contributions to humanity. But first much discord and dissension were brought to the land, and considerable discouragement to Ra-Ta.

In the meantime, King Araaraat (this being only one of his many titles) turned his attention to more industrious endeavours for the people, and a period of commercial activity began.

He drew the various races together and developed their abilities so that they might be used for the benfit of the masses instead of the classes. The rich material resources of the land were discovered. He opened mines at *Ophir,* later called *Kadesh,* in Persia, as well as in Abyssinia and other areas of the upper Nile country; he promoted the mining of such diverse precious stones as onyx, beryl, sardius, diamond, amethyst and opal. Pearls were taken from the sea near what became Madagascar. Stone cutting and polishing grew to be principal crafts for workmen. From other mines throughout the country, gold, silver, iron, lead, zinc, copper and tin were produced. Corn, wine, hides and jewellery were in common usage. Large granaries were constructed, as well as ships, bridges and viaducts. In *Deosho*, later named Alexandria, libraries were founded for the safe keeping of the greatest collection of manuscripts of the day.

From the wealth of the land, the King's palace and other state buildings of majestic splendour were erected. One of these was the Temple of Gold which was studded with enormous gems and panelled inside with highly polished woods of various colours. Its remains will one day be uncovered.

Storehouses, which also functioned as banks, were established as a means of exchange of goods and communications among the important nations of the world. These lands were Poseidia, the last of the great Atlantean islands; Og (Peru) in South America; the region of the Pyrenees Mountains in Europe; and what later became known as Sicily, Norway, China, India and America.

Only in Atlantis, where the Great Flood had broken up the continent into islands, had a division of tongues taken place. In other countries the people still spoke the one language. In Egypt itself there was one tongue but many dialects.

While the King was engaged in these pursuits and in political and social direction of the country, the High Priest Ra-Ta and his associates were busy setting up spiritual codes in conformity with the worship of the One God. The priest also helped to frame the civil laws for the penal and moral relationships of the people. New temples were constructed to house the activities for physical and spiritual rehabilitation of the masses.

Ra-Ta made frequent trips to Poseidia to study the methods and interpretations of those who remained faithful to the Law of One. In the city of *Alta* he met and discussed these matters with *Hept-Supht* (meaning "He who keeps shut"). An honoured and learned man, Hept-Supht was custodian of the records of many profound and secret religious tenets and laws which had been handed down from one generation to another in Atlantis. From Hept-Supht the priest learned a great deal about the problems concerning the mixtures as well as the Sons of Belial. Hept-Supht was anxious that the laws of the Children of One be preserved in Egypt.

Upon his return home, Ra-Ta immediately set plans in motion for the erection of two new temples: the Temple of Sacrifice and the Temple Beautiful. These two temples were thirty years in the building. The Temple of Sacrifice was a hospital or health centre; the Temple Beautiful was a school of higher learning and vocational training.

Some of the people of Egypt, as in other countries, were mixtures at varying stages of development. Large numbers were mentally, spiritually and physically inferior. Further complicating the social problems were the hordes of slaves who were still migrating from Atlantis with their masters, the Sons of Belial.

Ra-Ta hoped that the evolution of these creatures could be forced to the point where they would be stepped-up enough in spiritual vibration to enable them to act as thinking human beings, and not be at the complete mercy of their masters. This higher evolution would also remove their degrading influence from society.

Contemporaneously with these creatures, many people at a high state of evolution lived in the land; and it was the priest's plan to help these also in achieving a more rapid realization of spiritual at-one-ment with the Creative Forces. Thus they in turn might aid in the development of others less fortunate. An extensive training period was given, and these highly evolved ones were used to staff the two new institutions.

The Temple of Sacrifice was not only a physical but a spiritual hospital. Treatments for correction of deformities —bodily and mental—were accomplished not only through the use of surgery, medicines, electrical therapy, massage, spinal adjustments and the like; but by diet, the vibrations of music, colours, dancing, song, chanting, and most important, by the use of deep meditation in contacting the God force within the body. Both the patient and the priest or priestess assigned to the case took part in these activities. The objective was a purging of excessive carnal desires from the mental and of bodily defects from the physical.

There was also a process of purification involving the flames of the altar fires, and usually some six and a half years were required to complete the change of self-renewal. When the dross was burned away, the individual emerged as a progressed human being and soul, ready to begin the next stage of development. Because of the high degree of self-sacrifice in these ordeals toward the ideal of perfection in body and spirit, the human body came to be worshipped as something sacred, and a great deal of emphasis was placed upon its perfection and beauty. As the temple of the living God, it was indeed sacred, taught Ra-Ta.

The rejuvenation, however, was not always complete; in some cases as many as four incarnations in the earth were required to complete the change. Yet in a few centuries the mixtures began to disappear altogether from the face of the earth—an occurrence which would have taken place far less rapidly through rebirth and intermarriage with those of pure lineage.

These unfortunate creatures, the mixtures, were the ones which were portrayed so numerously in Egyptian, Assyrian, Greek and Persian art and hieroglyphics, and became the basis for legends of their existence in "mythology" thousands of years later.

From the Temple of Sacrifice, the patient graduated to the Temple Beautiful and to courses of vocational and spiritual training, recreation and rehabilitation. Here a highly specialized corps of priests and priestesses decided upon the type of vocation for which the student was best adapted—for his own good as well as that of society. An important decision was involved here, for it affected not only the present life of the individual but would have a bearing upon his future lives in the earthly cycle of progression.

Only the most highly developed and qualified men and women had the distinction of being chosen as instructors in the Temples. The status of the two sexes was equal; their dress almost identical—long flowing robes of handwoven material resembling linen but fabricated from the fibres of the papyrus and lotus plants. The colour combination was a striking white and purple.

Music in the Temple Beautiful was an essential part of

the course in raising the vibration and thought pattern of candidates to a degree that would enable them to become attuned to the Universal Forces through the "Silver Cord", or spinal column. Instruments such as the flute, lyre, harp and viola were used, and remains of some of these still lie buried in undiscovered tombs. Still to be discovered also are *seals* or *plaques*, emblematic of the soul patterns of persons who were in training.

The plaques were a sort of spiritual coat-of-arms, showing a series of scenes and symbols which served as a guide for the individual in adhering to the plan for his future development in the arts, crafts or professions.

Graduates of the Temple of Beauty went into many fields: agriculture, horticulture, music and singing, work in clay and pottery, in linen—including carding, weaving, and embroidering. Linen was made from cotton, hemp, papyrus and lotus fibres, and was of a higher quality than any attained since. There were no merchants at this time; there was one common store for everyone in this welfare state.

After the Temples had become firmly established, Ra-Ta gradually delegated authority to those he considered responsible and well grounded in the tenets of the law and sciences. He himself spent much of his time in travel in order to keep informed of the practices in other countries. Even when in Egypt he devoted a great deal of his attention to prayer and meditation, as did the Hindus later, with the ideal of developing a closer contact with the higher forces. As he entered more and more deeply into relationship with the Creative Influences, it was possible for him to attain unusual psychic abilities.

In virtual seclusion, he could be reached only through two or three persons close to him; and this fact coupled with the leaving of so much to subordinates, invited trouble from unsuspected sources. By the very reason of his trusting nature, the priest was totally unaware of some of the deteriorating practices which had spread throughout the land and had crept into the rites of the temples.

Certain leaders in the temples were being influenced by ambitious Atlantean political groups, and they considered the priest an obstacle in their desire for control. These temple authorities had conspired with those under them to bring about changes in practices, especially in regard to sex relations of the candidates—which heretofore had been restricted. Thus it came about that many who were dangerous and hostile to the spiritual significance of the worship began usurping power.

Upon Ra-Ta's return from one of his protracted journeys, he was shocked to discover so much loss in spiritual purpose of such widespread nature, when he had supposed steady progress was being made. The lusts of the flesh had become rampant; concocting of strong drink was prevalent; even blood sacrifices were being offered upon the temple altars which had always been devoted to offerings of fruits of the harvests.

An open break occurred when the priest unmasked those who had introduced such practices, and this precipitated a greater widening of the breach. The small but powerful group of enemies plotted the priest's downfall by another method, using the priest's interest in the idea of producing perfect physical beings.

In the Temple Beautiful was a native dancer of unusual beauty, grace and intelligence. She was regarded throughout the land as the most glorious and perfect creature yet to be born in Egypt—to such an extent that upon her death, years later, she was extolled as the personification of Egyptian beauty and perfection. Her name was Isris, later changed to Isis, and her memory was preserved in many statues.

As the daughter of the second sacrificial priest and a favourite of the King, Isris had access to the high priest, Ra-Ta. Pressure was brought to bear upon her to influence Ra-Ta to join with her to produce the perfect being of which he had long dreamed—thus subtly gaining tacit permission for those already perfected in body to procreate more rapidly, as the trainees' sex life had been limited.

Isris did not suspect the real motives of the instigators, and was tricked into becoming a party to the plot against the priest. And Ra-Ta did succumb to her unusual charms and the possibilities of the idea of their propagating the perfect being.

After Isris gave birth to the offspring of this union—a daughter named *Iso*—the politicians immediately exposed the high priest as the father and therefore the violator of one of the most important tenets laid down by the priest himself! *He* had written the law that no man should have more than one companion, and *he* had been the one to break the law.

The cry went up for banishment of the priest, and soon the country was split in a heated debate. As the lines of dispute were drawn, many arguments arose. The clamour was especially loud on the point of parents' keeping their children rather than turning them over to the state.

King Araaraat was torn between factions and faced with the task of deciding which was greater: the law or the maker of the law. Finally, after much mental torment and indecision, and considerable advice—some from the ones who were of the secret conspiracy—he issued the decree that sent Ra-Ta into exile. This was the first real division between church and state.

The place of refuge for the priest was the Nubian land, or what later became Abyssinia, south of Egypt. With him went 232 of his most devout and loyal followers, including Isris, Hept-Supht (who migrated from Atlantis), and many native Egyptians. The King kept the child Iso as hostage, and she died at the age of four years.

After the priest's banishment, internal strife nevertheless continued unabated. One faction consisted of the Atlanteans, many of whom were followers of Belial. These wanted to mould the young Egyptian civilization to fit their ideas. They disregarded the fact that the country was still in a formative state, and considered its civil and religious laws as inferior. What especially interested them was maintaining slavery of the mixtures, as they had done in Atlantis —and general docility of the people. With the removal of the high priest, the way seemed to be open.

Civil wars broke out in scattered parts of the country. The weapons of warfare were the sling and the projectile, the former often fastened to the backs of animals; and trained beasts such as bulls, leopards and hawks which were turned loose on the enemy. Transportation on land was by ox and cart; on water by raft.

Rebellions arose on religious as well as social and political issues—even involving the King's own household. The most significant disturbance was the *Ibex Rebellion,* and the King's handling of it demonstrated his long-range wisdom and compassionate handling of human problems.

Ralif, Prince of Ibex, was a younger brother of the King who had been given subrulership of a territory some distance from the Upper Nile country. Church and state representatives from both provinces were exchanged much as ambassadors are exchanged between countries. While the King was absent on a long journey, Ralif moved in on the palace and kidnapped members of the royal court, including the King's wife, *Osus.* Then he set up a separate southern state. When the King returned he found the capital in an uproar. A short but bloody war ensued and Prince Ralif was overcome. When the terms of the peace were made known, however, the people were astounded. King Araaraat restored his brother to his former position as governor in that part of the kingdom, and he allowed Ralif to keep Osus whom he loved and who returned his affection. Later years proved how ample had been the King's wisdom, for the Prince of Ibex became one of his most trusted and valued aides, as well as supporter of the priest's teachings.

During this revolutionary period a great deal of friction and dissension was also generated by a powerful Atlantean leader named *Ax-Tell* (or *Ajax*). He disagreed with the King in civil matters and with the Priest in religious matters—although in Atlantis he had been well-trained as a follower of the Law of One. He had high contempt for what he considered the inferior civil and religious conditions in Egypt compared with Atlantis.

But the most productive uprising came from among the Egyptians themselves. When the wave of rebellions was at its height, a native leader of the intelligentsia named *Oelom* organized an armed band to back up his demand for an audience with the King. When the opportunity to present his views was finally granted, he asked for the immediate recall of the High Priest Ra-Ta as the only one who could bring peace. The idea was supported by many of the dissenting groups, for stories about the Priest's remarkable achievements had been coming out of the Nubian land. When King Araaraat and Oelom finally settled their differences, realizing that their ideals were the same, a big step forward had been taken toward recall of the Priest.

What had been the achievements of the Priest in the Nubian land during his nine years' stay?

When Ra-Ta entered the land, the Nubian natives were a warlike and savage people. In nine short years peace and prosperity had been established; private homes had become the custom, and great advancements had been made in the knowledge of astronomy and astrology. Through studies made in deeply excavated caves, Ra-Ta had arrived at calculations which established what is known as longitude and latitude. He gained an understanding of the law which holds the heavenly bodies in place in the solar system, and the influence the sun exercises upon life; the effect of the moon upon the tides and the reason underlying the planting of seeds at certain phases of the moon. He came to believe that there is no time or space—that all force is One Force, and that man is the representative of the Higher Consciousness on the earth planet.

Those who shared the Priest's banishment also advanced in spiritual growth. Many worked through various channels of contact with those in Egypt who had access to the King and the Councillors, to arrange for the Priest's return. Hept-Supht, the Atlantean, had returned to Egypt after three years, and successfully maintained a neutrality which was of great assistance, for he was respected and revered by all and made many efforts to effect a reconciliation.

Thus at the conclusion of the Oelom rebellion, arrangements were made for the return of the Priest to Egypt. Those close to him in the Nubian land had been fearful that he would break under the strain which his activities had placed upon him at his advanced age. For Ra-Ta was now close to 100 years of age.

The announcement of the High Priest's recall brought rejoicing throughout Egypt. After an arduous journey from Abyssinia, the day came when the priest and his followers entered the royal city—a city lined with multitudes of cheering citizens in the broad highways, where colourful and fragrant flowers, bright green rushes and feathery grasses were strewn. Ra-Ta was both humbled and inspired that the faith in him had been so magnanimous.

The caravan from Abyssinia was made up of camels and other domesticated beasts, but also of vehicles constructed like chariots and propelled by the gases the Atlanteans had known so well how to control. In one of these vehicles sent by his Atlantean followers now in Egypt, Ra-Ta rode with

Isris, his companion. Other members of the Priest's family and those closely associated in the temple service rode in the remaining vehicles. In all, 167 souls returned to Egypt with Ra-Ta.

From that time forward, Ra-Ta was known simply as Ra. Isris was made Queen in her own right, and her name was changed to Isis. She became influential in working for the rights of women and in acting as an adviser to them, raising them in the social order. Years later she came to be worshipped as a goddess.

After many days of celebrating their return, Ra and the King met with other officials of the government and planned the amendment of certain laws and reorganization of the temple practices. The Temple of Sacrifice and the Temple Beautiful were cleansed of corruption and consecrated again to the worship of the One God. Segregation of family units into homes became firmly established, and the holiness of motherhood recognized. The revised law permitted a man to have more than one companion; however, such companions were chosen by the individuals and not by the government as before.

When insurrection disappeared, forts were quickly replaced by peaceful towns and villages, and a period of social and spiritual rebuilding was under way. With the establishment of a strong, centralized government in Luz, nationalism grew, and here began the first nation-spirit of a people. The King was once again in complete control of the political; the High Priest supreme in religious matters.

Aarat, the native adopted member of the royal family, who had previously been such a power with which to contend, was now subordinate to the King's will and his influences with the people reduced. An opportunity was thereby afforded others with ability for leadership to rise to positions of prominence and responsibility, and new ideas were admitted into the country's activities.

By this time, word had spread abroad concerning the wonders taking place in the new Egyptian civilization. Learned men from countries previously visited by the Priest now came to see and learn about the material and spiritual accomplishments. Emissaries were exchanged with the various lands of the world—those countries later known as China, Mongolia, India, Norway, Peru. This brought about an exchange of understanding and a correlation of civil and spiritual laws with other lands. In many directions, Egypt rose and took her place as a leader among nations, some of which were now declining.

A growing feeling existed among those in authority that the wisdom of this greatest of Egyptian cultures should be preserved in a safe place for the benefit of a new age yet to come. It became clear to Ra that it was his duty—and part of his purpose—to preserve the great truths that he had learned at such sacrifice to so many.

Furthermore, the records Hept-Supht had brought with him from Atlantis, together with the profound spiritual truths discovered by Raai, were considered invaluable. All leaders agreed that this body of records should be safely preserved somewhere against profanation by coming generations; until such time as man could again comprehend their significance. This would happen when the earth again changed its position on its axis, as it did in the Atlantean period, and pass through another inundation. According to the prophecy, this land change was sure to come.

The site finally selected for the safe-keeping of the records and for the great symbol of the esoteric content of the law, was the fertile plains of Gizeh, which stood firm during the flood that had swept over much of the land thousands of years earlier. This site was situated even higher than a Temple of Isis which had endured during that deluge. Also the area was conceived as being nearly the mathematical centre of the land of the earth, where there might be the least disturbance by future earthquakes or floods. Here the record vaults were to be hidden, in a small pyramid between the Sphinx and the Great Pyramid, and connected to both. Here, too, other large pyramids were to be erected.

The Sphinx had already been started; then work was discontinued; then restored and added to, after the return of the Priest. Originally it was intended to be a memorial to Araaraat, but after the recall of Ra the meaning was changed to symbolize the relation of man and the animal, or carnal world, to those changes which must come in his spiritual evolution—changes which were already coming about in the fading or falling away of imperfections of man's bodily pattern.

The base of the Sphinx had been laid out in channels, and in the corner facing the Great Pyramid the story was inscribed as to how all these were begun and built, giving the history of the first invading ruler and the ascension of Araaraat. From the right forepaw a passage was made to lead to the entrance of the Record Chamber, or Pyramid of Records. This was to remain undiscovered until man overcame his ego and reached true spiritual understanding, at the beginning of the fifth root race.

The Hall of Records was enclosed in a pyramid of its own, to stay hidden for many thousands of years. It is located between the Sphinx and the Great Pyramid. Hidden in the north-east corner were thirty-two tablets, buried with the remains of King Araaraat. This was the first of the pyramids to be constructed, and it will one day be uncovered from the shifting sands.

The Great Pyramid of Gizeh was one hundred years in the building; from 10,490 to 10,390 B.C. Ra himself made extensive studies of the terrain, and great care was taken in figuring the geometrical location in relation to the Sphinx and the four points of the compass. Although it was planned by Ra, the actual construction and engineering were worked out by Hermes, a descendant of Hermes Trismegistus, who had returned with the Priest from the Nubian land of exile.

The Great Pyramid was built as a hall of initiation, the "House Initiate" for those dedicating themselves to special services in the secrets of the mystery religion of Egypt. Here the masters performed their vows, consecrating themselves to holy service. Its purpose, therefore, was far greater than that of a burial place.

It was erected by the application of those universal laws and forces of nature which cause iron to float. By the same laws, gravity may be overcome or neutralized, and stone made to float in air. The Pyramid was thus built by levitation, abetted by song and chanting, much in the same manner in which the Druids of England set up their huge stones at a later period.

Material for erection of the Pyramid was brought from as far away as Nubia; many different kinds of stone being used. Highly polished, white limestone was placed on the four sides, in slabs whose joints were cemented together almost imperceptibly. This casing stone was later stripped off and pieces may still be found in buildings in Cairo. Portions lie buried below the sand. A few remain in place at the foundation line on the north side.

The Pyramid's capstone was composed of an alloy of copper, brass and gold, pounded into a covering for the top of the Pyramid. This also was desecrated, by the sons of Heth, on orders of the Pharaoh under whom the children of Israel suffered in bondage. In certain seasons a cosmic fire was lighted on top of the Pyramid, for symbolic purposes, by a method known only to the Atlanteans.

A long and elaborate ceremony marked the dedication of the Pyramid after the capstone was put in place. The event was announced to the people by a loud clanging of metal. From this ringing-out has arisen the call to prayer, thanksgiving and worship, as symbolized in the church bell. It is also the origin of the trumpet call to arms, and the ringing-in of the New Year.

The Great Pyramid is a record in stone of the history and development of man from the time of Araaraat and Ra to the end of the present earth cycle, in 1998. Its records are written in the language of mathematics, geometry and astronomy, as well as in the kinds of stone used, with their symbology. After the end of the cycle, there is to be another change in the earth's position, with the return of the Great Initiate for the culmination of the prophecies. All changes that have come and are to come are shown there in the passages from the base to the top. Changes are signified by the layer of stone, the colour of it, and the direction in which the turns are made. There are no undiscovered rooms, as such, in the Great Pyramid.

In the smaller Pyramid of Records, yet to be uncovered, there is a vault sealed with heavy metal, containing the prophecy for the period from 1958 to 1998. Here were secreted the records of the people of the One God from the beginning of man's entrance into the earth. The occasion of this sealing was attended by Araaraat, Ra and the priests and priestesses of the temples.

In the Great Pyramid current history is symbolized by the low ceiling at the entrance of the passage leading to the King's Chamber. This low passage or depression shows a downward tendency, as indicated by the variations in the kind of stone used. The present period, therefore, may be termed the Crucitarian Age, or the age in which preparations are made for the beginning of the new sub-race. Astronomical and numerical factors indicate this date began in the Autumn of 1932.

When the gradual change taking place in the position of the North Star, Polaris, becomes noticeable as calculated from the entrance of the Pyramid, there will be clear evidence of the incoming of the new race, with a greater influx of souls from the Atlantean, Lemurian, La, Ur or Da civilization. These conditions are indicated by the turns in the passage through the Pyramid. The empty sarcophagus in the King's Chamber is itself a symbol of the enlightenment of man as to the meaning of death—as a transition from one plane of existence to another.

The length, breadth, height and various directions of the many layers of stone in the passages and chambers of the Pyramid depict accurately the events of significance in the spiritual evolution of man in the earth plane. The birth and death of Jesus of Nazareth are indicated to the year, day and hour, at the turn of the passageway leading to the Queen's Chamber.

At one point in the low passage, 1936 is prophesied as a year of disturbances and turmoils, including wars, storms and land upheavals, with a resulting unrest among groups and masses. After 1956 a time of adjustment follows, and then the world enters a new period as shown in the King's Chamber—some time between 1938 and 1958. This era is the beginning of developments of an unusual nature in many ways, terminating in the year 1998. It will be a time of *preparation* for the coming of the Master of the world —not necessarily His actual coming, the time of which no man knows. It will be a period of great spiritual reawakening and enlightenment; of new understanding, new life and new faith. There will be marked advancements in the field of science and new knowledge concerning the balancing of the forces of gravity by which the Pyramid itself was built.

The present age of mankind is rapidly approaching a peak in its development. At the crest of the wave there will be a breaking, a clash between the material-minded and the spiritual-minded. Many will fall away, but those who stand firm will be guided in finding the records and interpreting them for the benefit of men everywhere. The important thing is not just their discovery but their correct interpretation.

The Great Pyramid of Gizeh stands as an historical monument to the present root race. It records the story of man's struggle for spiritual wisdom, and for many ages it was used as a temple of initiation for the world's great teachers and leaders. It was here that the Great Initiate, Jesus who became the Christ, took the final Initiate degrees, along with John the Baptist, His forerunner.

At the age of 104, King Araaraat passed away and was buried in the north-east corner of the first pyramid built during his reign of eighty-eight years. The High Priest Ra lived to be several hundred years old according to the method of computing age.

It had been a remarkable rule in many ways; one of turmoil and peace and progress, of social and spiritual enlightenment. Together Araaraat and Ra had brought the country into closer understanding with the other nations of the world. Together they had raised the standards of their own people to a new high, materially and spiritually. They had fostered a civilization that was to be the greatest expression of Egyptian culture for a long time to come. But most important, they had inspired man's first real search for God among a heathen people

Today man stands again at the threshold of a new era— the Aquarian Age of mass consciousness or awareness, a new world unity.

Extracts form the Cayce Readings

"As Amululu, the entity was among the Atlanteans who came into Egypt, coming among the children of the Law of One to make preparations for the preservation of the tenets and truths that had been handed down by the teachers. This made for an interpretation of those truths dealing with the relationship of man to the Creative Forces. In application of their dealings with their fellow creatures may be found that which is the soul's own true relationship to its Creator, within its own experience. This is an inversion of what He gave: 'As ye do it unto the least, ye do it unto me.'

"In that experience the entity was of assistance in those activities dealing with the correlation of the teachings from the peoples of the land now called the Indian, or the land of Saneid, the land of On, and the people from the Mongolian land; as these gathered . . . for the correlation of the best in each, that these (truths) might be applied in the lives of the peoples. They sought to make greater and greater manifestations in dealings with their fellow man, and their activities brought them into closer relationship and understanding with the Creative Forces.

"There at the first of the entity's activities we find these making for a depletion in self, through . . . the things that man so oft worships, that are made by his own hand. These we find moth and rust do corrupt; for change of attitude, change of environ, change of ruling influences cause such to fade away. Modes and manners may change but the purposes remain, for as He gave, 'The heavens and the earth will pass away, but my word and deed—and kindness and loving thought, patience, persistence in the right—do not pass away.' These are the foundation stones upon which nations rise that seek to know God. These taken away make for those destructive forces that have arisen and do arise when man has forsaken God and turned rather to a god of greed, a god of gold, a god of stone, of fame or of fortune. These fade and die but the deeds, the kindness, the gentle words remain forever."

(Case # 1159)

"The entity was among those who were keepers of moneys, corn, wine, skins and precious stones; and the one close to the King who rose in power during that experience. The entity gained, for not only did the entity make for better relationships with the peoples in the various lands round about . . . but the entity prepared the channel through which the understanding gained was carried to other lands.

"There may still be found in the pyramid not yet uncovered that which was accomplished during this period; not only the entity's seal of the King, but the entity's own personal seal bearing the dove and the horns of the ram.

"In the present we find many of these same people, and many have become associated together. Also there exists the urge for a return of man's more perfect understanding of the divine laws which have been made manifest through the various ages of evolution of man in this plane. And the indwelling forces will be of assistance in gathering such together."   (Case # 261)

"The body was worshipped then as sincerely as most of the . . . spiritual worship today; for bodies were changing in form as their developments or purifications were becoming effective in the temples. These bodies gradually lost, then, feathers from their legs . . . many lost hair from the body, gradually taken away. Many began to lose their tails, or protuberances in various forms. Many paws or claws were changed to hand and foot, so that there might be more symmetry of the body. Hence . . . the body became more erect, better shaped to meet the various needs.

"Those who had achieved such transformation, to be sure, were considered to have the body beautiful—beauty as something divine, for the divine has brought and does bring such various beauties of form or figure to the body; for 'the body is the temple of the living God.' "
                                        (Case # 294–L–8)

"In structure, as this (the Temple Beautiful): There had been gathered from all the nations of the earth that which represented from their environ and surroundings the most beautiful gift, that this might be a reminder to those who purified or gave themselves in service there, the *beauty of service* of every land in this preparation of the bodies. . . .

"The materials used, outwardly, were from the mountains nigh unto the upper waters of the Nile. It (the Temple Beautiful) was in the form of the pyramid, within which was the globe . . . which represented to those who served there a service to the world.

"The furnishings may be surmised from the fact that the most beautiful things from each land were gathered there: gold, silver, onyx, iron, brass, silk, satins, linen.

"As to the manner of the service there: The individuals, having cleansed themselves of those appendages that hindered, came not merely for a symbolic understanding. . . . There were first the songs, the music, as we have indicated that ye sing . . . which makes for . . . the vibrating with light—that becomes colour, that becomes tone, that becomes activity. . . .

"With the music came then the dance, that enabled those having disturbing forces and influences to become more erect and upright in body, in thought, in activity.

"Then there was the giving of the seal of life by the Prophetess, that was set upon each and every one who passed through these experiences—(showing) how or in what field of activity were the individual's relationships to its fellow man, in maintaining material existence; being *in* the world, yet not *of* the world. . . .

"The teaching, the preparation, the ministering, the song, the music, the activities that give expression—these arise in man's experience from those activities in the Temple Beautiful."   (Case # 281–25)

"With the political situation, then, the King—the young King, then only thirty—gathered about him many who were to act in the capacity of council; a portion to be the inner council that ruled on the general circumstances of the people as a whole; then the council that had supervision over various parts or departments of the activities of the people. This as would be termed in the present day surroundings, as . . . various offices of a cabinet, the departments being in that day much as they are in the present. For remember, there is nothing in the present that hasn't existed from the first. Only the *form* or the manner of its use is changed. And many an element was then used, the art of the use of which has been lost; and many are being rediscovered by those called scientists in the present, all of which in that day were common knowledge of the most illiterate, as would be said in the present.

"With this giving in . . . of the King to parallel activities of the natives . . . there was the necessity for matching the abilities of the King's Council with facilities of the natives . . . in various phases of what would be termed *progress* in the present. Hence the opening of mines by Araaraat; mines in Ophir, in what was later known as Kadesh, or in the land now called Persia. Also in the land now known as Abyssinia (and those portions yet undiscovered in the upper lands of the river Nile) there were mines for precious stones—as onyx, beryl, sardis, diamond, amethyst, opal—and the pearls that came from the sea near what is now called Madagascar. In the northern (or then the southern) land of Egypt, there were those mines that produced quantities—and quantities, and quantities—of gold, silver, iron, lead, zinc, copper, tin and the like. . . . Also there was the producing of stonecutters who began gathering materials for the residences of the King's peoples. . . . Also Ra-Ta began to gather his own people and those pointed out to him . . . for the establishing of the name forever in the land. Hence with these there were preparations for the temple where there would be various forms of worship. . . ." (Case # 294–L–13)

"As the monument called the Pyramid of Gizeh was being built in the plains, this entity superintended building or laying the foundations. He figured out the geometrical position of the Pyramid with relation to the buildings which were put up or connected with the Sphinx.

"The Sphinx was built in this manner: Excavations were made for it in the plains above where the Temple of Isis had stood during the deluge which had occurred some centuries before. . . .

"The base of the Sphinx was laid out in channels; and in the corner facing the Pyramid of Gizeh may be found the wording of how this was founded, giving the history of the first invading ruler and the ascension of Araaraat to that position." (Case # 195–L–2)

"The sojourn of Araaraat in Egypt was 11,016 years before the Prince of Peace came into this land. We find that this was one of the highest civilizations of Egypt since it has been in its present position. For it had been submerged for nearly a quarter of a million years since civilization had been in that portion of the earth. . . .

"Araaraat drew the people together and developed their abilities so that they could be used for the benefit of the masses, rather than classes. . . . Many titles were given to him in the various dialects of the people. But Araaraat is the one that will be found recorded, with those of the other rulers." (Case # 254–39)

"As respecting the pyramids and their purpose in the experience of the peoples, in the period of the rebuilding by the Priest during his return to the land—some 10,500 years before the coming of the Christ into that land, there was first the attempt to restore and add to what had already been begun on what is called the Sphinx, and the storehouse facing same, between this and the Nile, in which records were kept by Arart and Araaraat in that period.

"Then with Hermes and Ra . . . there began the building of that now called Gizeh . . . that was to be the Hall of the Initiates of that sometimes referred to as the White Brotherhood. . . .

"In this same Pyramid did the Great Initiate, the Master, take those last of the Brotherhood degrees with John, the forerunner of Him, at that place . . . as is shown in that portion when there is the turning back from raising up of Xerxes, as the deliverer from an unknown tongue or land and again is there seen that this occurs in the entrance of the Messiah in this period—1998. . . ."

(Case # 5748–5)

"This, then (the Pyramid) holds all the records from the beginnings of that given by the Priest, Arart, Araaraat and Ra, to that period when there is to be the change in the earth's position, and the return of the Great Initiate to that and other lands, for the fulfillment of those prophecies depicted there.

"All changes that occurred in the religious thought in the world are shown there, in the variations in which the passage through same is reached, from the base to the top —or to the open tomb *and the top*. These (changes) are signified both by the layer and the colour and the direction of the turn."

(Case # 5748–5)

"In those conditions that are signified by the way through the Pyramid—as of periods through which the world has passed and is passing, in relation to religious or spiritual experiences of man—the period of the present is represented by the low passage or depression showing a downward tendency, as indicated by variations in the kind of stone used.

"This might be termed in the present as the Crucitarian

age, or the age in which preparations are being made for the beginning of a new sub-race, or a change which—as indicated from astronomical or numerical conditions—dates from the latter or middle portion of the present fall (1932).

"The Dipper is gradually changing, and when this change becomes noticeable, as might be calculated from the Pyramid, there will be the beginning of the change in the races. There will come a greater influx of souls from the Atlantean, Lemurian, La, Ur or Da civilizations. These conditions are indicated in this turn in the passage through the Pyramid. . . .

"Q–8. What is the significance of the empty Sarcophagus?

"A–8. That there will be no more death. Don't misunderstand or misinterpret! The *interpretation* of death will be made plain."   (Case # 5748–6)

PART TWO

THE LOST PEOPLES
OF AMERICA

Chapter Five

ENIGMA OF THE INCAS

Man is said to have colonized North and South America from Asia during the long paleolithic phase of his career on earth. It is not possible to date the migrations precisely, but they may have begun about 25,000 B.C. The route supposedly went by way of a land bridge or ice bridge now covered by water in the Bering Strait off the tip of Alaska.

In so far as the word *race* has meaning in relation to the diversity of human beings, the migrants were evidently Mongoloid. As farming had not yet been practised, they were hunters, and doubtless it was in pursuit of game that they endured the long journeys. There was no single great migration. For century after century small parties of men, women, children and their dogs simply drifted eastward into North America. Some moved on south to Mexico and beyond. Probably by 10,000 B.C., they had reached and spread themselves over those parts of the Andes Mountains in Peru which, where habitable, offered game and wild vegetable foods.

Archaeologists have peeled back the centuries of Peruvian history and found a succession of cultures dating to perhaps 9,000 B.C. But unfortunately, we have no history of these pre-Inca civilizations. Not one had writing; there were no dated coins, in fact, no money. Even their names are not known for certain; they're simply called Early Hunters. There are no "talking stones" as found among the Mayas of Central America, no definite time element until as late as A.D. 1527, when the Spaniard Pizarro came to Peru and conquered the modern Incas, the most progressive, advanced people of all South American Indians.

Much of what we know comes from sixteenth-century records of the conquerors. One of their manuscripts, *The First New Chronicle and Good Government*, was not uncovered until 1908, in the Royal Library at Copenhagen. This valuable history wasn't published until 1927.

But of the Early Hunters, we know almost nothing. Even the name "Ohums", found only in the Cayce readings, has apparently been lost in antiquity. Carbon-14 tests date the *Chavin* culture as early as 3000 B.C., but man had already been on the north coast of Peru for millennia. What little is known of the Chavins, a place name for lack of a better one, comes from designs on textiles, ceramics, structures and their architecture.

Tradition has it that the early Incas came from Lake Titicaca in southern Peru, wandered north to the valley of Cuzco in the Andean Mountains, and established their empire. This has been confirmed by archaeology, but some scholars dispute the origin, insisting they must have come from outside, conquering the many small tribes of different speech, customs and legends. Yet all had the same plants under cultivation, used the same crude hand tools, and had domesticated the llama, their largest beast of burden.

Interestingly, one of the older cultures, the *Chimú*, has *mu* as its last two letters, reminding one of the people of Lemuria, the Mu. The Chimú culture stretched for six hundred miles along the Pacific before it was subdued by the Incas from the mountains. They excelled in weaving and pottery.

Preceding the Chimús by several centuries were the *Mochica* people, who constructed an adobe pyramid 800 feet long, 470 feet wide, and 200 feet high. According to tradition, chambers and passages were secreted there, one containing the body of a mighty prince. The early tribes believed they were descendants of birds and animals, and that many years ago strangers had come from over the seas.

Pre-Incas worked in textiles and pottery, buried their dead, and apparently were not a war-like people. They built their shrines and pyramids. But one of the puzzling questions is, who built the walls across the mountains? Called the "Mysterious walls of Peru", one runs for 50 miles inland, is 15 feet wide and about the same height. Constructed of stone and adobe, they are of uncertain date and origin.

The Incas themselves have a tradition that the earlier people were invaded from the south, driven to the hill country where they set up a superior civilization, and eventually built the great Inca Empire. There is evidence some of them migrated to southern Mexico and fused with the Mayas. There is also recently discovered evidence that the Mayas drifted southward and mixed with the Incas.

The controversy over the origin of the Incas is an interesting one in the light of what the Cayce records have to say on the subject. Some evidence has been found that the Incas may have migrated to certain Polynesian islands, in the Pacific (*Kon Tiki,* by Thor Heyerdahl). But the reverse was also possible—that early Peruvians were originally from Polynesian lands.

On the other side of the debate, the excavations of Dr. John Rowe indicate the Incas were native to Peru. "Enough had been done", he writes, "to show that the Inca civilization *was* a product of a long development in the valley of Cuzco itself and that consequently it is unnecessary to look farther afield for that civilization's cultural origins." (*Inca Culture at the Time of the Spanish Conquest*)

The *Quechuas,* a tribe of the Inca people, were Indians of the red race and with an appearance and trait which is distinctly American. "They are", says Victor W. Von Hagen in his book, *Realm of the Incas,* "of medium height, and inclined to be thickset, with large hands, small wrists, a disproportionately large chest (developed for breathing at high altitudes), well-developed legs, and wide-spreading feet. They are broad-headed, with high cheekbones, prominent aquiline noses, and small, almond-shaped eyes." There are still five million of them living in the Andes.

Largely a treeless area, they adapted themselves to their environment and used what was at hand—stone. Superb stonemasons, like the Mayans in Yucatan, Mexico, and the early Egyptians, they too built pyramids, temples, walls, baths and other structures without mortar. The stones are so closely fitted together that a knife blade cannot be inserted between them. Their work is unmatched in modern times yet parallels the craftsmanship of the Mayans and Egyptians.

The early Peruvians lived on the coastal plains and in the foothills of the Andes. Man, like other creatures, is constantly influenced by his environment; consequently, at least two—perhaps more—quite different kinds of human communities developed. The coastal plains are rainless deserts crossed from east to west by a series of mountain rivers, and these streams created fertile valleys along their courses. The valleys provided a habitat for hunting man since there were game animals. But South America is not very rich in game, and the species are small. The valleys also nourished flora for food gathering—the collecting of roots, seeds and fruit.

In due course it probably occurred to some that certain plants could be grown at home instead of being sought far afield; seeds dropped by birds or excreted in dung may have shown them the way. In a short time, the valleys, because of the shortage of game, forced the Early Hunters to invent gardening, and therefore agriculture. A fundamental creative act of American man was the development of maize. For it was maize that made possible and sustained the whole Peruvian civilization as well as Mexican and Central American ones. Exactly where it originated is not known, but corn was found in pre-Mayan graves dating to 3000 B.C.

Under the later Inca professional farms, the whole of the realm from the coast to the upper Amazon River became a flowering centre of plant domestication. More than half of the foods that the world eats today were developed by these Andean farmers. More kinds of food and medicinal plants were systematically cultivated here than in any other area of the world. Among them are potatoes, squash, tomatoes, beans, peanuts, peppers, papaya, cashews, pineapples, chocolate, avocadoes, mulberries, strawberries. So many and so varied the plants, and so long domesticated in the Old World, that one forgets all of these originated in the Americas.

While excellent farmers, the early Peruvians and their descendants were also making progress in crafts. "An important characteristic of all Central Andean peoples was great manual skill associated with very simple apparatus, a feature which they shared with other South and Central American peoples," writes G. H. S. Bushnell in his book, *Peru: Ancient Peoples and Places.* "Their weaving was unsurpassed and is particularly characteristic of the area. They applied most of the known techniques, using both cotton and wool, on a simple back-strap loom. Pottery was skillfully modelled and painted, producing vessels of great artistic merit, but the potter's wheel was unknown. Gold, silver, copper and their alloys were worked by a variety of processes, and the production and working of bronze was finally mastered. Among the useful metals the most obvious absentee was iron, which was unknown anywhere in America." Wood-working, basketry and stone masonry were skillfully used on a large scale.

The hold of religion on the Indian was enormous; life was practical and religion was real. His fate was controlled by the all-pervading, unseen powers and he had to come to a tacit agreement with the gods, for his own well-being, he believed, depended on them. Although he had many gods, only one, the creator-god—*Tici Viracocha* —was very real. There were many lesser gods; and these had special functions and powers. In death, the little man had to be content with the little gods. His end, like his beginning, was a simple ritual. He believed in immortality; indeed he believed one never died, for after expiring the dead body merely became undead and took on the influences of the unseen powers.

In pre-Inca Peru and during the Imperial Inca period itself, the law had religious sanction to such a degree that it is not always easy to distinguish crime from sin. They were, apparently, much one and the same. But dishonesty and serious crime seem to have been a rarity, perhaps because of the socio-economic system, as we shall soon see. The Inca people had a creation story and a flood story, migrating from one *Aztlan.*

Sun worship along with moon worship—the moon being the sister-bride of the sun—was the apparent religion of the Incas. When they conquered the Andean world they could not impose their religion on all the people of the empire, if only because their authority was based on their direct descent from the Sun God, who was used by the great Animator to breed Incas. They studied astronomy, geometry, music, philosophy.

Another concept of God, under the name of *Pachacamac,* was a high and noble one. On the surface, Pachacamac means simply Creator of the Earth, but the name probably expresses a much subtler and more imaginative idea and feeling. According to Garcilaso de la Vega in *The Incas,* the word means "He who does to the universe what the soul does to the body." As least one Spanish

cleric claimed that the Indians had a trinity of God the
Father, God the Sun, and God the Moon.

Many sun temples and sundials were built, cared for
by the priesthood. There was a hierarchy, and the pontiff
was a close relative of the ruling *Sapa Inca,* the High Inca.
A person who had done evil purged himself by confession
of "Sins of word and deed" to a priest in public. The sinner
was given a penance to do and was required to purify himself by washing in running water, evidently a form of
baptism and repentance. Divination was practised, oracles
were consulted, and animals sacrified. It is certain that
human sacrifice, too, was practised in pre-Inca times.

Economically, the Inca system resembled a socialist
state. "All the means of production, distribution, and exchange were in the state's hands," write Hyams and Ordish
in their volume, *Last of the Incas.* "At the same time, the
country was extremely flourishing, and the worst evil of our
own world—grinding and degrading poverty—was completely unknown. It seems certain that this social system
was a product of the physical conditions under which the
Andean nations ultimately united in the Inca empire . . .
The geology, the soils, the climates of the whole region were
such that large and ordered communities . . . could be
created only by people working together under strict discipline, and to a plan.

"Our system of free enterprise in Western Europe and
North America was a product of inexhaustible and readily
accessible natural resources; we (in the person of our
ancestors) were in a position to squander natural wealth
and we could therefore afford to limit cooperation and
specialization well short of social conscription. But the
Andean peoples could not; their communities could grow,
their wealth could accumulate only if they built and
operated vast irrigation systems and continually increased
their farm lands by mountain terracing on a colossal scale.
And the only way to accomplish such works, since these
people—although they were remarkably fine artists and
craftsmen and natural engineers—were technically in the
early Bronze Age, was to combine in a tightly organized
society."

The *allyu* was the basic social unit of the Incas. A cooperative or collective system, it seems to have been indigenous throughout the Andean region. It was upon this cooperative principle that the Inca empire was built.

The allyu was a clan of families, a tribe, living together in a specific, restricted area with a common sharing of land, animals and crops. There was no private ownership of property. Every Indian was born in an allyu, large or small —from village to large city. Even Cuzco, the capital, was only an enlarged allyu. But the Incas did not invent this communal system. It was already there, part of a heritage from primitive Andean society. The Incas, however, did systemize and extend it.

Each allyu was led by an elected leader and guided by a council of elders. Several of these communities came under a district chief; a number of districts formed a territory, headed by a sort of governor who answered to the Royal Inca himself. Land was divided between church, state and allyu.

Politically, the system was essentially theocratic socialism. Economically, it was basically pyramidal. At the bottom was the *puric,* an able-bodied male worker. Ten workers formed a group supervised by an elected straw-boss; ten straw-bosses chose what might be called a foreman; ten foremen in turn picked a supervisor, usually the head of the village. The leadership continued in this fashion to the chief of the tribe—composed of up to 10,000 workers. The governor of the province and the rulers of the "four quarters" of the empire were appointed by the Sapa Inca at the apex. For every 10,000 workers there were 1,300 leaders, supervisors, officials.

Normally, an Indian was born, lived, and died in his allyu; it was his principal and primary loyalty, suggesting a high level of spirituality. An individual would have to be religiously mature to place the good of his community ahead of his own personal gain; to cooperate rather than compete with his fellow man. The first Christians, the Essenes, with their Christian communism, had much the same social structure. But today in Peru some fifty Spanish families still control much of the land despite reforms and the nationalization of some industry. The natural resources of gold, copper, silver, vanadium are no longer entirely dominated by foreign investors, mainly North American.

The Inca civilization reached its height about A.D. 1000, and after the bloody conquest of Pizarro in his search for gold, dissolved about 1600. Some of their descendants believe they are the world's oldest people. They still pay homage to the sun, hold ancient, colourful festivals, animal dances. Remnants of their high civilization remain, including parts of their paved road system, which, oddly enough, contained steps. The purpose and use has never been determined, unless as is likely with the Mayas, as we shall see, the highways were built mainly for religious processions.

From the Cayce Records

One of the first lands to which the fleeing Atlanteans migrated during the upheavals was what is now Peru, then called *Og, Oz,* and *On.* This was the only large area of South America above water, and it was already occupied by a tribe of brown people known as the *Ohums,* or *Ohlms,* who were of Lemurian origin.

Lemuria had sunk into the Pacific Ocean with the first cataclysm. The Ohlms had come from the south when the lowlands went under, about 50,700 B.C. They set up their communities to the north, established their homes, estates, and Temples of Mu. There were priests, priestesses, ministers, teachers, "workers and shirkers" in this earliest of Peruvian cultures.

A peaceful people, they found themselves in a land rich in natural resources of gold and precious stones, and they soon became highly skilled craftsmen in these trades. They also excelled in music, art, braiding of beads, and jewellery for bodily adornment. Religion was more than a matter of belief, it was a way of life, and some of them had a thorough understanding of man's relation to the universe. In the Temple of Mu only the best of the fields and the flocks were offered as sacrifice.

The people were .uled by a line of monarchs, at least one of whom was a woman, who were known as the High Ohlm. But during the last rule an insurrection by the people succeeded in establishing new democratic principles of self-government. Although the revolution brought some pain, bloodshed, persecution and hardship for a time, it marked the birth of a new socio-economic system. The new rule was to have significant and far-reaching influence on future systems of government throughout the world. Indeed, their "principles of self-government have gone to the best rule through many, many ages". There were still classes and castes, but there was a new, just division of wealth among "the well and the ill, the strong and the weak". Predictably, there were some who disagreed with this philosophy.

With the coming of the Atlanteans and the people from the "South country" of On and Og, many changes again took place. The Atlanteans came from the remaining islands of Poseidia and Eizen Land in the north, Aryaz in the east, and Latinia in the south, and not only to escape the water but to avoid the civil war between the Children of the Law of One and the Sons of Belial. Those of both camps sought out the high lands of Peru, together with people from the south, thus compounding an already complex situation.

At this time the land of the Ohlms was ruled by a weak leader who degraded himself by his sexual excesses. The invading Atlanteans brought conflict and bloodshed, but they succeeded in overthrowing the High Ohlm and sent him into exile, an action that brought popular approval and helped in solidifying the country.

The Atlanteans immediately exerted their influence in the government and the economy of the land as well as in religious thought. More modern methods of cultivation of the soil and new devices for the mining of minerals were introduced. New temples were erected along with the establishment of new rituals and chants with much rote and ceremony.

In political affairs, the idea of the welfare state—"the care of the least and the lowest"—was developed and expanded upon. The general welfare of the populace was paramount, for Inca chiefs were in fact trustees and managers rather than "rulers". Castes were eliminated, and "all were of one abode" and equal. Common storehouses were set up to meet the material and educational needs of the people. Yet, as always, there were some Atlanteans who, seeking wealth and self-aggrandizement, were ready to put their fellow man "under bondage".

Eventually there came a breakdown in the morality of the Incas. Sun worship crept in, and human sacrifice. The hoarding of gold and precious gems led to their use as media of exchange. Ambitious individuals of the Sons of Belial seeking power and authority corrupted even the religious temples.

Yet new products continued to come into use and old ones improved upon; fine linen, raised needlework, basket weaving, pottery, metals. Gold, copper, and valuable stones were mined in quantity, adding to the wealth of the nation.

Atlanteans from Central America continued to come into Og and On for many years, with considerable travel back and forth between Peru and Yucatan. The native Ohlms gradually gave way to the influx. There was a mixing of brown and red races as well as cultures and tongues. Yet out of this melting pot of humanity rose the great Inca nation. It was the Incas who built the "conduits", the "walls across the mountains", and they dominated the land up to the very edge of recorded history.

Thus the coming of the Atlanteans brought about the end of the Ohlms and the beginning of the Incas. Some Ohlms fled the country and entered Yucatan, where they helped to set up the new kingdom of the Mayas there with the Poseidians coming into that land. A few migrated as far north as Southwestern United States—Arizona, New Mexico, Nevada—and fused themselves with the cave- and cliff-dwelling Lemurian and Atlantean elements of that area. But as a people, the Ohlms vanished from the face of the earth. Historically, nothing is known of them by that name today.

Extracts from the Cayce Readings

"In the one before this we find that land now known as Peru. The entity was then among the Ohlms that gave much to the peoples of that day in the way of converting the elements of the earth to the use of man. Hence jewellery, precious stones, and those things that glitter attract unusually the entity in this present experience; yet the hoarding of same is abhorrent." (Case # 2731–1)

"In the one before this we find in that land known as the Peruvian, during the period of the Ohlms, before the Incas and the peoples of the Poseidian land entered. The entity was then a princess in this land, and a ruler or a co-ruler with those who made insurrections, and those who later brought much persecution on the peoples through the furnishing of that for the gratifying of selfish interests; yet the entity high in mind, high in development—not losing, not gaining in soul's development through the period."
(Case # 1916–5)

". . . in the Peruvian land, before that, we find the entity was overzealous because of others who had a WAY! The entity considered self and not the general welfare of the peoples as a whole." (Case # 949–11)

"Before that we find the entity was in that land now known as the Atlantean, during the periods when there were the turmoils after the first outburst—or the separation of the isles and the land. The entity was among the people that were with the Sons of Belial, that warred with the sons of the one influence—or the forces that are known as the relationship of man with the Creative Forces that may be manifest in the earth. Yet with the destruction there was the gaining activity because of the influence in the experience that in the present would be termed good. When those divisions again came, the entity was among those that attempted to leave the land for the sojourning in other lands; bringing eventually those activities in what is now known as the Central American land. In the experience the entity became in the latter days of sojourn, in those active forces in what may be termed the Incal land, the second in command; becoming the priest in the latter portion of its sojourn." (Case # 670–1)

". . . in the land that now may be called the Peruvian, during those periods when there were the persecutions—not those known in the much later date as from the

Spaniards, but rather from the breaking up from the meetings with those from the Mayan or Yucatan land.

"There we find the entity was in the capacity of a priest, or the son of the ruler or the High Priest; yet never attaining quite to the period in that experience of being one wholly in authority. Yet the entity was acquainted with much of the various groups' activities; not only as to the general welfare, where there were the universal storehouses from which all gained or had issued to them the needs of the bodily forces, but as to the mental and spiritual applications as well. For that was the type of government during the period, and the entity's activities were to keep such a storehouse—when there were the intentions of activities of those within the entity's own household as well as others to become rather as lords, and as those who were willing to put the fellow man under bondage . . .

"Before that we find the entity was within that same Peruvian land, though not exactly in the same territory; rather in that from a part of the Atlantean as well as a part of what became later the On or the Incal land . . . and in the activities of those of the Children of the Law of One. There we find the entity was very, very well adapted in the activities for the meeting of the influences of a great variety of the groups. For the entity was rather the adept in the various tongues, by the activities of the various groups. As these were a part of the entities' experiences, we will find the abilities in languages—or in the various inflections of what may become colloquialisms, or local conditions in groups of peoples—may be of special interest to the entity in the present sojourn."   (Case # 1637–1)

"In the one then before this, we find in that land known as the Peruvian, and when there was the end of the Ohums and their rule over the land. The entity was among those that came from the Atlantean lands and gave to the peoples much of the impulse of the added forces in a practical building up of material things of life, as pertaining to court hangings, ritualistic forces, the adding-to by the entity then of the worship to the sun and the solar forces, even to that of the offering of human sacrifice; for the entity was the first high priestess to the sun in the land, making the first human sacrifice in that period. Losing and gaining through a service rendered, yet these that must come as sacrifices —have come as sacrifices in the present that the entity itself has made—have been met in *many* a manner. Then in the name *Rariru*." (Case # 2887-1)

". . . we find the entity was among those peoples in the land now called the Incal land, but among those who came from other lands into that land, being among those who were called the invading peoples.

"Though we find the entity's choice was not to cause death or destruction merely for the gains of gold or those things pertaining to those peoples, the entity was overruled; which caused much in the experience that brought discouraging activities.

"And this has created in the present experience of the entity a horror of things that cause fear, or that have been the outgrowth of barbarism or the like as related to individuals taking advantage or using the activities of others for selfish motives or for the aggrandizement of appetites within the experiences of such. Not that there is not an awareness of these by the entity, but the purposes, the aims, the desires—which arose from that sojourn in portions of the land now called Central America, as well as in the Incal land—brought determinations, activities, longings for such activities in which—while all to the entity might not be upon an equal basis—all might be equally considered in their sphere, their scope, their abilities for activities."

(Case # 2147-1)

"In the experience the entity was a priestess, in those interpretations of what later became known as the Incals, the Lost Tribes, the peoples from the Atlantean land, the peoples who came west from the activities in the Lemurian land. All of these became as a portion of the entity's activity . . .

"The experiences during that sojourn make for the greater influences in the present. For metals, glass, crockery, woven cloth, the use or application of these in the services not only for the places of abode but for the places of amusement or for places of worship, these the entity insisted upon as its activity of separating as one from another.

"These in times past, or in the experiences of many, were all as of one abode. The entity made for a separation, yet these brought for its very self, confusions."

(Case # 1159–1)

CHAPTER SIX

THE AMAZING MAYAS

Of all the countries to which the Atlanteans migrated, none reveals their influence so much as Yucatan, Mexico. Here is the most marked example of Atlantean culture super-imposed upon an earlier, simple tribe of people. Fortu-nately, a great deal is known of the Mayas, from both the standpoint of science and the Cayce readings.

The history of this southernmost peninsula of Mexico has long puzzled modern archaeology. Indeed, the riddle of the Mayas has provoked the imagination of man ever since Hernan Cortes conquered the remnants of their civilization in A.D. 1541. Within a century they had all but disappeared, a fact as mysterious as their origin.

Who were these people? From where did they come? What caused their sudden growth from a primitive people to a cultured civilization? Why did they constantly move to new and unfavourable areas? What became of them? These are the questions that perplex historians. We shall examine the findings of science and then turn to the Cayce readings for further enlightenment on the known as well as the unknown.

Explorers have uncovered much of the Mayan civiliza-tion, for it left a wealth of evidence, although not all of it is deciphered and evaluated; but of the Mayas' origin and movements, almost nothing is known.

The marks of the Mayan culture are numerous: already discovered are some of their "books", lofty pyramids, mas-sive stone temples with intricately sculptured altars and thrones; huge, one-piece stelae—round, shaft-like monu-ments weighing up to 65 tons—and even courts used for games similar to basketball.

That the Mayas were far ahead of their time there is no doubt, so much so that they were destined to become known as "The Greeks of the New World," says S. G. Morley, an authority on the Mayas. Indeed, "theirs was the most brilliant expression of the ancient American mind". Their talents in sculpture and architecture were equalled by their highly developed systems of hieroglyphic writing, mathematics, astronomy and governmental administration.

They were the first to use the zero in arithmetic. Masters of mathematics, their method of chronology was more accurate than the old world system used at the time America was discovered. It is so complex and delicately built that it is difficult for scientists to believe that the formula was developed piecemeal over a long period of time. Rather, it seems to have suddenly become full-blown and the work of a single mind or group of minds, perhaps around the third century B.C. Unfortunately, archaeologists have never been able to correlate it with any known historical event, which prevents the dating of the period. Too, their complicated hieroglyphic writing has more than 600 characters, of which only half have been deciphered. Unhappily, the Spanish destroyed most "books".

Because they were an agricultural people, the seasons were important in their planting and harvesting times. Their astronomers therefore recorded the various movements and phases of the planets, much of which is also of unknown significance.

Of the earlier Mayas, it is thought that they may have come here from Asia some 12,000 years ago. Unlike the modern Mayas, they left no documentary sources and only fragmentary tradition of their first history. There is a total absence of architecture or other traces of large-scale building. So little is known that they are simply titled "Pre-Mayan".

From what is known, they were apparently a simple, peace-loving, religious people, worshippers of one God. Although they had a number of lesser gods, called *Bacabs*, their supreme Deity and creator of the world was a God named *Hunab Ku*—meaning "One God". According to legend, they arrived in Yucatan from two directions: by way of the Gulf of Mexico and overland from the south and west, led by a hero named Zamna, a sort of Moses. They had another tradition that incorporated the existence of several civilizations before them, all of which were destroyed by a deluge. Little else is known of them.

Yet archaeologists found the later modern civilization superimposed upon the old. This strange occurrence is believed to have taken place about 1000 B.C. Something fundamental did happen rather suddenly in their growth. Exactly when and what happened no one knows, but Morley, in his book, *The Ancient Maya*, asks, "Was this quickening of the cultural pulse due to some outside influence?"

In *Gods, Graves, and Scholars*, C. W. Ceram states that so often has he found the kernel of a legend historically validated that we must not make the mistake of dismissing them as mere poetic invention, however fictitious they may appear at first sight. The most prominent supporter of the Atlantean theory was Edward H. Thompson, who for twenty-four years was U.S. Consul in Yucatan. Interested in archaeology and the Mayas in particular, he rarely saw the inside of his office. He died in 1935, still convinced the Mayas were from the sunken continent of Atlantis. A few others have held to this view despite long sighs of dismay among the conservative element.

There is evidence that the Mayan civilization is much older than at first supposed. Striking similarities to ancient Egyptian art are in abundance, and lava taken from a pyramid near Mexico City was judged by unsuspecting geologists to be 8,000 years old. If correct, it would place the Mexican culture 1,000 years earlier than the Old World of Babylonia, Greece, or Egypt. This so upset the archaeologists' scheme of things that they tended to regard the geologists in error. Ancient cultures are known to exist beneath the present Mexico City, but are unreachable.

There is no question that *something* happened in the Maya's growth, and to add to the puzzle ample evidence has been found that for some unknown reason there were numerous later migrations of the Modern Mayas. They simply picked up and moved on, abandoning their crops, temples, and cities *en masse*.

Many highly speculative theories have been offered in explanation of this: civil war, foreign conquest, deterioration of the soil, religious superstition, plagues, encroachment of the jungle, earthquakes and climatic changes. Entire populations of cities in the south deserted their homes and moved into the western portion of the Yucatan peninsula, where jungle growth was a problem, the soil poor and unsuited for the cultivation of maize, their principal crop, and the water supply almost non-existent. But with these movements began the modern history of the Mayan people.

The new empire built over the old is entirely different and so marked that there is no question but that the Mayas found an earlier people in Yucatan. In addition, Mexican infiltration downward in the tenth century A.D. further complicated the Mayan civilization. Most importantly, it is thought to have brought numerous gods, idolatry and human sacrifice.

There is a Mayan tradition that their pioneer entry into Yucatan was from the east and at first only in small numbers. This was called the "Lesser Descent". Later they came in large numbers, and this was named *Nohenial,* or the "Great Descent". The legend is significant, and there is some corroboration of it and the inland movements in the discovery of earlier dates in the eastern communities than in the western.

One of the earliest and most spectacular discoveries of Mayan cities is that of *Copan* in northern Honduras. John Lloyd Stephens, a young New York lawyer, and Frederick Catherwood, an English artist, penetrated the jungles by mule pack and found a majestic city of monumental buildings and artistic sculptures. They bought the site, in 1839, for fifty dollars, and began excitedly hacking away at the overgrowth covering their find.

In a few weeks, they uncovered eleven stone stelae with sculptured figures and hieroglyphic inscriptions, carved heads of jaguars, shrines, terraces, courts and pyramids. The edifices were joined by sweeping flights of stairs, one decorated with some 2,500 glyphs. Stephens hoped these would one day reveal the "entire history of the city". Unfortunately, most of them still defy interpretation.

The two explorers went on to find a total of forty-four Mayan cities in southern Mexico, including some of the most famous sites: *Palenque, Uxmal, Chichen Itza.* Later Stephens was to write:

"We did not find on either the monuments or sculptured fragments any delineations of human, or, in fact, any other kind of sacrifice, but had no doubt that the large sculptured stone invariably found before each 'idol' was employed as a sacrificial altar. The form of sculpture most frequently met with was a death's head, sometimes the principal ornament, and sometimes only accessory . . ."

In 1938, in *Uaxactun*, Yucatan, S. G. Morley uncovered a pre-classic period pyramid from underneath another temple mound. The beautiful stone structure, coated with white plaster, was ascended by staircases on four sides, between which were rows of Jaguar masks in stucco. The latter bore the markings of "Olmec" style, a Polynesian-type people believed by some to be older than the Mayans.

Perhaps the most startling and unexplained find was that of a giant, five-ton, limestone drum. Now broken in two, it was some thirteen feet long and two feet in diameter, and looked like a huge road roller. Its purpose has never been determined, although the Mayans did build roads of stone, cement and stucco. Indications are that a whole network may once have covered the land. The people are known to have had wheeled vehicles if not beasts of burden, once disputed.

One explanation is that the roads were used solely for ceremonial processions. "One can visualize", writes Thomas W. F. Gann, "the gorgeously arrayed procession of priests and nobles setting out from Cobá, their jewels, bright-coloured garments, and magnificent feather head-dresses glittering in the sun, preceded by singers and players on the flute and drum, and followed by white-robed priests, bearing grotesque censers, scattering the sweet-scented smoke of burning copal incense." After three days' march, they would reach their mecca, the castillo at Chichen Itza, where they would be met by priests of the great Plumed Serpent, and make their solemn offerings of sacrifice.

Unhappily for us, the Mayas were more interested in astrology and astronomy than they were in history, so little of it has been found. But the Mayan *Book of Chilan Balam* records their culture and gives a detailed account of a great catastrophe in the earth. There is other corroborating evidence in Mexico of volcanic eruptions, earthquakes, and tides destroying early cultures.

Their religion was closely associated with the calendar, which in turn had a great bearing on crops. The calendar was equal to that of the Egyptians and far superior to that of the Europeans. Their religion was a pragmatic one. The population was divided into priests, nobles, and warriors on one side and the common people on the other. In between was the merchant class. Large numbers of priests were required for the ministering to the numerous gods, most of whom personified the earth. Of these, four were of most importance, one of which was the chief God who ruled over the other three and the rank and file of the lesser gods. He was the Serpent god, *Kukulcan,* and was a sort of messiah. In their modern religion were strong Christian elements, including the symbol of the cross.

The chief priests officiated at only very special functions, spending most of their time in teaching the younger priests. There were regular priests known as *Chilans,* special priests called *Nacons,* and below them lay-priests named *Chacs.* Their duties varied with their rank, and they were democratically elected by the village for a term of one year, after which they were replaced.

In addition to the priests there were groups of young maidens who were responsible for the housekeeping of the temples and courts and maintaining the sacred fires. These were women of high rank and were recruited on a voluntary basis.

There is evidence that the Mayas practised human sacrifice, but usually animals, birds and fruits were offered to the gods. These sacrifices almost always concerned crop conditions, such as rain, sunshine and bumper harvests. Altars and sacrificial stones are in abundance, but their hieroglyphics are mostly untranslated.

To summarize briefly, the Mayan civilization reached its zenith by A.D. 200. Inexplicably it declined about 600 and disintegrated after 1600 with the Spanish conquest.

From the Cayce Records

Perhaps the real story of the Mayas properly begins in Lemuria and Atlantis with the first land changes. At that time there were the beginnings of the moral decay within Atlantis that eventually brought dispersion and annihilation to a "proud, wicked, adulterous people". Materialism, wars within, self-indulgence, and the misuse of spiritual knowledge and power were their undoing. Some of the

Atlanteans were aware of the coming catastrophe and sought to gather all the knowledge and wisdom of man to combat it. A high council was held in 10,700 B.C., without result.

The first upheaval, with the shift of the poles which brought the last of the great Ice Ages, had already occurred. Lemuria, lying in the Pacific Ocean and bordering what is now the west coasts of North and South America, began to sink. The continent of Atlantis was broken up into several large islands and the southern portion sank altogether.

Migrations to Yucatan from Lemuria began with the first cataclysm, but it was not until the second, the Biblical flood, in 28,200 B.C., and the third, in 10,600, that the great exodus from the principal remaining Atlantean islands of Poseidia, Araz, and Og took place. These movements toward the visible portions of Yucatan, then called Yuk, thus occurred over an era of many thousands of years. In the later periods some came by aircraft.

The peninsula of Yucatan was quite different from what it is today. Instead of being flat and tropical, it was much larger, more temperate in climate, more varied in topography. It was during the third and final land upheavals that it became changed to its present outline, losing much of its territory in the process and forcing many of the inhabitants inland.

Thus there was a merging at wide intervals of time of the red race from Atlantis in the east with those earlier settlers of the brown race from Lemuria in the west and Peru to the south, and mixing of many faiths and cultures. Further complicating the cultural scene, some of the early inhabitants of southwestern U.S., Israelites of the Lost Tribes of Egypt, later drifted as far south as Yucatan, bringing with them, among other things, their metals and clays. As a result, more than one civilization has been and will be found as research progresses. The Mayas too, led a communal life of "all for one, one for all".

With the beginning of the exodus to Yucatan, the Atlanteans took with them the common knowledge of their great civilization, but not all the technology. They could not, of course, at any time transplant it in its entirety, but they were intensely interested in preserving some of their culture and learning, especially the religious tenets of the Law of One.

They expressed their influence at once in the building of their cities. This was manifest in the magnificence of their temples and courts, their astute form of government and keeping of records, their knowledge of agriculture, mathematics, decorative art, precious jewels, and textiles.

"Before that the entity was in the Yucatan land, when there were those establishings of the peoples who had escaped from Atlantis.

"There we find that clothing and things pertaining to precious jewels were of special interest to the entity; the *decorative art*, and this applying to certain characters of *textiles*, also was a portion of the activities.

"For the entity then, while not the individual in authority, was of the same family; in the name then *Tep-k-eux*. In the experience the entity gained, and while disagreements arose among many of those because of the differences in opinions as to the application of the spiritual laws, these the entity brought better in control than most of those through that particular period." (Case # 1'664–2)

Later they took up the practice of cremation, the ashes of which may yet be found in one of the temples constructed for this purpose.

Many of them were priests and priestesses, for they were particularly interested in their religious studies and their many rituals. The Temple of Light (Sun), since uncovered, was the principal centre in their lives and around it revolved much of their activity.

The first temples built by the Atlanteans were abandoned in the final disaster, and their remains have been discovered. The pyramids of the earliest culture have also been uncovered but not all opened, although attempts are being made to recognize the real connections and associations. They were built by the lifting forces of those gases which we are gradually learning about in the present.

There may also still be found in the ruins the influences of the Egyptian, Lemurian and Peruvian cultures. Many of the second and third civilizations may never be discovered, for it would destroy much of the present Mexican one, mainly Mexico City, to uncover them.

The giant circular monuments of stone, or stelae, were of the earliest Atlantean period. These had a definite place in their religious services; indeed they were symbolic of the Spirit of the One God. The altars were used for the cleansing of bodies of individuals (monstrosities?) of hate, malice, and selfishness, not for human sacrifice. This came much later with the injection of the Israelite influences. The pyramids and altars were the work of the peoples from Og and Mu—Peru and Lemuria—referred to in the scriptures as the high places of family altars or family gods.

The Peruvians also brought destructive influences; religious arguments arose creating dissension, causing many Mayans to emigrate to southwestern U.S.A.

"The entity was among those who journeyed to other lands, knowing much of the activities of the Sons of Belial as well as the precautions and warnings that were issued by the children of the Law of One.

"Hence we find the entity was among those who in the early portions of that material sojourn entered into the new buildings, the new activity that became destructive because of the influences from the land of Og and On, and the activities that arose in the western portion of that particular period of sojourn.

"For there, during the entity's experience, was the upheaval which settled so many in portions of that now known as the Southwestern U.S.A.

"In the experiences then the entity rose to that position of the priestess of the sacrificial activity. Much blood flowed by the hand of the entity during that sojourn." (Case # 1604–1)

It was in 3000 B.C. that the wandering people of the Lost Tribes of Israel came down from southwestern United States. Their ancestors had reached that land from Egypt by boat via Lemuria. Drifting southward through Mexico to Yucatan, they infused their activities upon the peoples from Og, Mu, and Atlantis, including the practice of human sacrifice, which brought much bloodshed.

"Before that we find the entity was in the Egyptian land when there were preparations of individuals for activities in other lands. The entity was among those who were prepared in the Temple Beautiful for those activities in what is now Yucatan." (Case # 3384–3)

Later sun worship crept in and sun god drawings and markings were made on walls and buildings before the Spanish conquest in the sixteenth century.

In Yucatan still lie undiscovered many of the secret records of the history and culture that will one day explain the truth of their heritage as well as some of the early accounts in the Bible. These same tenets are also locked in the depths of the Atlantic and in the Egyptian pyramids. Mayan altar stones, predicted to be uncovered in 1938, and of which so little is known by historians, are part of these records. They will eventually end up in "Pennsylvania State Museum, Washington, D.C., or Chicago".

Today some 3,000,000 of the Mayas' descendants still survive in scattered parts of Yucatan and Guatemala. In the latter country, a truly feudal state, 2 per cent of the population owns 70 per cent of the land. The Mayas, mostly illiterates, earn up to 80 cents a day on the banana plantations.

Tourists now travel by bus and train to sites of excavations first hewed out of the jungle by hand-wielded machetes. The city of Chichen Itza is the most extensively recovered Mayan metropolis. Here are located the great Temple of the Warriors and the Castillo, largest of the pyramids. It is 190 feet by 230 feet at the base and 60 feet high, considerably smaller than the Great Pyramid of Egypt but larger than the earthen mounds of the Mound Builders in central United States.

The work still goes on. The National Geographic Society, National Science Foundation, Carnegie Institute of Washington, University of Pennsylvania and United Fruit Company have sponsored expeditions which uncovered new cities and temples. Yet much remains to be discovered and understood about the strange tribes of Indians known as the Mayas.

The Edgar Cayce readings do not discuss by name certain other Mexican cultures, such as the Toltec, Aztec, and Olmec civilizations, but by implication. They therefore play part in our story.

In Deuel's *Conquistadors Without Swords,* we find "Again and again waves of nomadic tribes from the north swept into the Valley of Mexico, replaced earlier settlers, acquired some of the amenities and cruelties of civilization, and were conquered in turn. Hence its rather chequered and turbulent history, which makes it so challenging an area for the student of Mexican antiquities." Our next chapter touches on this very subject. The great disparity is in the dating of the various periods, which scientifically are at best uncertain. The oldest Mayan city supposedly dates back to only 1500 B.C.

The Olmecs, a strange, shadowy people, were of a physical type foreign to the racial features of the known peoples like the Mayas. The latter were Indians, the former more Polynesian or Ethiopian in appearance, according to their sculptures. We can only ask, Who were the "Olmecs", and where did they come from? What were the meanings of such features as jaguar men, baby faces, human freaks, bearded strangers? They appear to be even older than the Mayas, yet somehow related to them, for alien influences on the Mayas are in abundance. Question: were the Olmecs of Lemurian origin? Did memories of the monstrosities follow them to Mexico?

About one-half of all Mayan hieroglyphic signs have been deciphered, and some of their stones are now at the University of Pennsylvania Museum in Philadelphia and the Chicago Natural History Museum, as Cayce predicted. Russian experts say they have cracked the code, but promised full translations have not so far appeared. Exciting revelations may yet come from the Mayas.

Extracts from the Cayce Readings

"In the one before this we find that land now known as the Central American land, or Yucatan. The entity then among those who journeyed to this land in the building up and establishing of a new kingdom there from the trembles of the Atlantean land, though the entity journeyed from that now known as the Peruvian, or the land of the Ohums."   (Case # 170–31)

"Then, with the leavings of the civilization in Atlantis —in Poseidia, more specifically—*Iltar,* with a group of followers that had been of the household of *Atlan,* the followers of the One—with some ten individuals—left this land *Poseidia* and came westward, entering what would

now be a portion of Yucatan. And there began, with the
activities of the peoples there, the development into a
civilization that rose much in the same manner as that
which had been in the Atlantean land. Others left the land
later. Others had left earlier. There had been the upheavals
also from the land of Mu, or Lemuria, and these had
their part in the changing; or there was the injection of
their tenets in the varied portions of the land—which was
much greater in extent until the final upheaval of Atlantis,
or the islands there which were later upheaved, when
much of the contour of the land in Central America and
Mexico was changed to that similar in outline to that which
may be seen in the present.

"The first temples that were erected by Iltar and his
followers were destroyed at the period of change physically
in the contours of the land. That now being found, and a
portion already discovered that has laid in waste for many
centuries, was then a combination of those peoples from
Mu, Oz and Atlantis."   (Case # 5570–1)

"The entity was in the Atlantean land, during the periods
when there were many of the divisions that called for and
produced the destructive forces in that land. Yet when
there were the expressions of those in power to raise those
who were of the menial class, or the workers in the fields of
activity that brought what is known as the agricultural or
the social service, the entity was the intermediator for the
peoples of the lower class or caste to those of the higher . . .

"The entity was not among those to be sent to the
Egyptian land, but rather among those that went to the
western portions of the land and eventually to that known
as the Yucatan and the Central American land; for in those
sojourns the entity was active in establishing a development
in the agricultural field, or the growth of those things that
made for the sustenance in the new land."

                                          (Case # 801–1)

"Before that we find the entity was in the Atlantean land,
during those periods when there were those activities that
brought about the last destruction of same through the
warrings between the children of the Law of One and the
Sons of Belial.

"There the entity was among those who waned between the children of faith or the Law of One and those who sought the use of the spiritual forces for their own self-indulgences, self-aggrandizements.

"The entity was among those, though, who were sent to what later became or is in the present the Yucatan land, of the Mayan experience.

"There the entity rose to one of power; yet with those very wavering experiences there was not always peace brought to the entity." (Case # 1599–1)

"Before that the entity was in the Yucatan land when the people settled there who came from Atlantis. The entity was a priestess among those who set up a form of activity there; being also then associated with records that were attempted to be *preserved* from the old order of things in Atlantis.

"We find that the entity established and added to, or detracted from, the circumstance decided upon as the expedient one for the change in clime and in surroundings." (Case # 3590–1)

"The entity was among those who were sent as the directors to what became the Yucatan land, and in the setting up of the temple and the temple service, the temple of worship, the temple of differentiation in the labourer and the ruler.

"Then in the name *Ikunle,* the entity made for a great service to a great people; that made for the bringing about of the preservation of much that may some day make for a unifying of the understandings as to the relationships of man to the Creative Forces." (Case # 1426–1)

"Before that the entity was in the land now known as or called the Poseidian land, or Atlantean land, during those periods in which it was breaking up, and then the Children of the Law of One (to which the entity was enjoined) journeyed from the land into portions of what is now the Yucatan land.

"The entity then was a Princess in the Temple of the Sun, or the *Temple of light;* though others have interpreted it as the Sun.

"There the entity made overtures not only to its own peoples but to those of many other lands that there be the activities of the peoples in bringing a greater knowledge of the association or relationship of the creatures in the earth to Creative Forces, as indicated in their activity with others.

"There the entity was in splendour, yet sorry for the disturbing forces in so many of those lands roundabout."

(Case # 2073–2)

CHAPTER SEVEN

THE FIRST
NORTH AMERICANS

Long before Atlantean colonialists or Mayan emigrants reached Arizona and New Mexico and fused themselves with primitive tribes, there existed here a vastly different climate, flora and fauna. The Southwest therefore plays a part in the panorama of the forceful and enterprising Atlanteans and their descendants.

Geology dates the first ice age at about one million years ago, when much of the United States was inundated by glaciers. The last glaciation occurred some 10–12,000 years ago, once believed to be before the advent of man here. No evidence has yet come to light in North America linking man with any ape forms. Because of this, the Old World has long been regarded as the home of the human race. Scientific inquiry into the origin of the American Indian is therefore most concerned with how and when man reached this continent.

The *Amerinds* are thought to be much younger than European man but older than Central and South American man. They supposedly came from the Mongols of Asia about 10,000 B.C., crossed via the Bering Strait which was then a land or ice bridge between the two continents, and drifted southward to western U.S. and eventually into Mexico and Middle America. From there some of them apparently migrated back to Southwestern U.S. and on to the Midwest.

In the then fertile region of Arizona and New Mexico, they took advantage of their surroundings—the natural shelter offered by cliffs and caves and the native clays for making sun-dried bricks. Some, known as the Cliff Dwellers, later developed a complex and distinct culture. The modern Pueblo Indians are their descendants.

In the Midwest, where the early Indians are believed to have lived from at least 3000 B.C.—perhaps 7000 B.C.— to A.D. 1000, they set up a very different civilization, although they appear to be related. Here they became known as the Mound Builders.

John C. McGregor in his book, *Southwestern Archaeology,* states that the earliest known, relatively well-dated cultures in the Southwest are some 13,000 years old. From about 10,000 years ago to the present there is much more abundant evidence of man in the area, indicating greater numbers and activity with a more consistent development from one stage to the next.

As there were still ice sheets in the northern part of the West and Midwest 11,000 years ago, there can be no doubt that man existed in this country at least during the later period of the Ice Age. Most of the early sites, however, have been found in the South and Southwest, well outside of the ice area.

There are numerous sites on the eastern fringes of the Southwest which were occupied primarily by hunters, though they may also have done some gathering of foods such as berries and fruit. Carbon-14 tests show that the Sandia and Clovis, New Mexico, types of remains date to about 10,000 B.C. or earlier; other evidence suggests 20,000 B.C. One carbon-14 test of charcoal ashes found in Nevada indicates an age of at least 23,800 years. New evidence from hearth stones uncovered in California's Mojavi desert reveals man lived there 100,000 years ago.

The early Southwesterners were basically hunters of big game. Most of the finds of their cultures are in what are called Kill Sites, i.e., places where large game animals were killed and butchered. The lance-like projectile points used are the most common and distinctive artifacts, and these crude but effective tools have been carefully studied, classified and named. There are subtle differences in shape and fluting, indicating different makers of different tribes at different times.

Characteristic features of the early desert culture point to sparse populations in small, migratory groups who lived in caves and built grass beds. As seasonal gatherers, they harvested small seeds and, as always, fully exploited their natural environment. They made basketry, cordage, netting, matting, and fur cloth from animals. Their hunting implement was the spear with hardwood shafts and stone points. They also had flat, curved, wood clubs.

By at least 7000 B.C., they used flat milling stones for grinding small seeds in basin-type stone receptacles, along with scrapers, knives, and similar tools. Later they seem to have become less nomadic, building permanent structures of stone and adobe.

The Early Man stage can be subdivided into three parts. The first, from perhaps 23,000 years ago to 10,000 B.C., produced the first known evidence of man in the area. At this latter time the ways of life in northern New Mexico and the desert culture of southern Arizona seem to be most marked. The next period, that from 10,000 B.C. to possibly 5000 B.C., called the Hunter Period, saw a significant elaboration of these ways of life and what appears to be an increased occupation of the Southwest. The two groups were still distinct but each had developed more diversified tools and more skillfully made artifacts. Some still lived in cliffs and caves while others appear not to have done so. In the last, the Collector Period, from 5000 to 200 B.C., the emphasis seems to have shifted more to the development of the southern desert culture. Domesticated plants, such as corn, were introduced during the latter part of the period, and the way was opened for the spectacular growth of later times—the Hohokams, who had a game similar to basketball—and other pre-Columbian groups.

The modern Indians of the Southwest are the descendants of these earliest Americans. Remnants of the numerous tribes—the Ute, Navajo, Apache, Hopi, Zuñi, Papago, Pima and others—all different yet somehow related, still exist. For the most part, they reside in adobe huts on reservations set aside by the Federal government from the least desirable and productive land. They have never integrated well with Whites or Spanish-Mexicans, and indeed, show no desire to do so. Their historical significance, for our purposes, is that they were at the crossroads for transient tribes from the west, north, and the south; and were the connecting link between the Mayas and the Mound Builders of the Midwest.

One of the most important discoveries of the early desert culture was that of a kill-site near Naco, Arizona-Mexico, in 1952. Remains of a mammoth and eight spear points were recovered from the bank of the San Pedro Valley's Greenbush Creek. The find helped to prove that early hunters killed and feasted upon animals which no longer exist, and of a size that required heavy foliage for their sustenance. The climatic history preserved in the earth around the site is a reliable and widely used clue in establishing the date. Dr. Ernst Antevs, a leading specialist in this study, has placed the Naco find in a period between 11,000 and 10,000 years ago. This would indicate these bronzed, black-haired, loin-cloth girded hunters trapped their prey at about the time of important land and climate changes.

But the oldest substantial find is Sandia Man, so named for a cave discovered in the Sandia Mountains near Albuquerque, New Mexico. He lived some 20–25,000 years ago. Buried under layers of dust, silt, clay and limestone were bones of horses, camels, mammoths, bison, wolves and other animals. Ashes and hearths, along with an assemblage of all kinds of hand tools made of stone, were clear signs that the butchered creatures had been dragged into the cave for barbecuing. The stratification at different levels was plain. Now dry, the cave at one time had been dripping with moisture, indicating the lush times of the glacial period when mammoths were extant. The Sandia people were among the first North Americans, at least of record.

Later came the Basket Makers of the desert culture, and finally the Cliff Dwellers of Mesa Verde fame in Colorado (A.D. 1000?). The long narrow skulls of the former are distinctly different from the broad skulls of the latter, suggesting entirely different races of people. The longheads appear more Australoid than Mongoloid, and some scholars believe them to be North America's first immigrants.

It is obvious that the ancient Southwesterners lived in a much different environment than that of today, and that they preyed on a whole menagerie of Tertiary creatures, from mammoths and mastodons to native American horses and sabre-toothed tigers. Undoubtedly, new finds will continue to be made, but so far the oldest shows 37,000 years of age, from carbon-14 tests of Clovis spear points found near Lewisville, Texas.

Although the early Southwesterners had some things in common with Central and South American man, there are singular differences; they built no earthworks and raised no permanent temple platforms. Their creation and flood stories are similar to those found in other parts of the world, including migrations to high land. They, too, evidently had little violence, crime, warfare. Modern American Indians for the most part maintained no military forces until the coming of their white conquerors. Living communally, there was little cause for quarrels over property rights. The land was simply there for the free use of all; no one "owned" it; it belonged to the Great Spirit.

There is only slight evidence of Israelite influence among Indian tribes. Hebrew metal and stone engravings have been found dating to the first century A.D. *In the Mountains and on the Plains,* David Meriwether, governor of Arizona-New Mexico Territory in 1853–57, writes: "The missionaries in this country, and other learned divines, have a theory that these Indians (Navajos) are descended from one of the lost tribes of Israel, as all the figures on their blankets resemble the pyramids of Egypt, and the instruments used in making these blankets are precisely the same as the pictures of these instruments in the old English Bibles, which are spoken of in the Bible as the "Distaff and Spindle" used by the Jews.

"In addition to this, they do not bury their dead but place them in caves in the mountains, which brings to mind the cave of Machpelah and others spoken of in Jewish history. But the question arises, how did any of the lost tribes of Israel reach the continent of North America?"

The Navajos differ in many ways. They treat their women with greater respect, are cleaner in appearance, and the women hold personal property such as sheep and wool separate from their husbands, although the Navajos have long lived communally.

Interestingly, the Hopi's have a snake dance similar to that of the Mayas, and a legend embracing three previous worlds of existence. The first world was a life of living with the animal kingdom, of becoming corrupt and being destroyed by fire. In the second world, they developed handicrafts, homes and villages, but upon becoming decadent it was overcome by ice and water. The third world produced large numbers of Hopi's, great cities and a whole new civilization. But the people became so materialistic they were destroyed by water, a few alighting atop a mountain. In the fourth and present world, after many migrations, they came to the Southwest where they lived in cliffs and caves. Here they could once again choose to conform to the plan of Creation or have it too destroyed. Tradition has it that their migrations were from west, not from the north.

In the Northwest, we find the totemism of the Hupa and Kato Indians of Oregon. Totem poles originally represented animals held sacred as the sign or symbol of the tribe, clan, or individual. In Australia the Emu clan of aborigines believe themselves to be descendants of the emu, a native animal which they hold sacred. Totem poles exist in Polynesian, Asian and African countries among others, with only slight variations from the Oregon type of half human, half animal figures.

This most confounding of associations persists back through the ages to ancient Egypt and Assyria, and, according to Cayce, to Atlantis and creation itself.

At some unknown date the Mayas found their way to the Southwest, he said, but their impact, except on religion, appears slight compared to the other countries we have examined.

From the Cayce Records

A quite different picture of the earliest North Americans, although there are many similarities, emerges from the Cayce files. When man first appeared in the earth in the five simultaneous occupations by the five races, the land of Southwestern U.S. was the only large area of the continent above water. Lower (Baja) California, comprised the coastland of Lemuria, where lived the people of the brown race. Utah, Nevada, Arizona, New Mexico and parts of Mexico along with the great continent of Atlantis were inhabited by the red race. "Indians", then, were native to the Southwest.

The first Americans made their homes in the cliffs and the caves, from which they later derived the name Cliff Dwellers. They practised polygamy, although some adhered to the principle of one mate. Metals were used as media of exchange and for bodily adornment. Iron was one of the first discoveries, and it was quickly adapted to practical use. Earthenware and line drawings were their chief arts, and in these they soon became proficient. Soothsaying, magic, stone carving and the making of beads were prevalent.

In 50,722 B.C., a meeting of the five nations or races was called to formulate ways and means of combating the enormous, carnivorous beasts threatening man in so many parts of the world. At a later period emissaries were sent to join in a similar council held in Egypt and to another in Atlantis concerning the coming upheavals in that part of the world.

The first North Americans also set up temples of worship and very early instituted a semblance of organized religion. With the first land changes, which resulted in the sinking of Lemuria, some of the people of Mu escaped to Lower California, Southwestern U.S., as far north as Oregon and as far south as Peru. In Oregon may be seen remnants of their religion in the totem pole, their family tree. Here the women were the head of the family and ruled rather than the men.

With the great flood, in 28,000 B.C., Atlantis was broken up; some Atlanteans made their way by Mexico to the highlands of the Southwest and the "land of Mayra —Nevada and Colorado". Many were religious emissaries of the Children of the Law of One to what they considered a strange people. Their objectives included the extension and preservation of the laws of the one God. There were also immigrants from Yucatan and as far away as India, who were known as the "Happapulpick people". They were proficient in metals and clays. Later some of the descendants of the Lost Tribes of Israel also found their way here by boat from Lemuria. There was, then, a great influx of peoples, especially to what is now Arizona.

Say the readings: "The joining in the activities there were for the attempts to establish with those peoples that had been a portion of the lost or strayed tribe that came across from Lemuria; as well as with those that came from the lands of bondage by the Persians and those that later were called the Indo-Chinans—or those peoples from the mountains who raided the Indian land. There the entity aided in establishing a new unison of activity in what would now be called the Arizona land." (Case # 1434–1)

By the end of the last debacle, 9500 B.C., the mixed cultures of the Southwesterners was a complex one indeed. Moreover, in 3000 B.C., many of them were driven farther south by the "heavy men" from "the north", and they took with them their abilities in metals and clays as well as the practice of human sacrifice, which the Israelites had originally brought from Egypt. In Central America they exerted their influence on the Mayan Indians of Yucatan, but centred most of their activity in the Valley of Mexico, or Mexico City.

The reference to the "heavy men from the north", unexplained, is an intriguing one. The answer may lie in the widely accepted theory that Asiatics (Siberians?) did at one time enter this continent via the Bering Strait, but apparently only in small numbers. The theory is circumstantially based on geography, geology and ethnology, but almost no concrete archaeological facts. It is indeed possible, for as one authority writes, "we find in Alaska a race of big men," and therefore different from those we have been studying. What is improbable is the populating of the Southwest by that route.

The early Americans were, as elsewhere, a highly religious people with many signs and symbols, says Cayce. "For the peoples understood—even better than they do today—how that the heavens declare the glory of God, and as to how nature sings His praises in the rebirth at each period, each cycle, for its unfoldment and growth. . . ." (Case # 2438–1)

From this mixture of ancient peoples, then, descended the great variety of American Indians found by the white man when he arrived in this part of the North American continent. The brown round-heads of southern Arizona are still distinguishable from the red long-heads of other regions.

The most revealing facet of the Southwest's pre-history is that the area was the native land of some of those of the red race from the time of creation. Man was here from the beginning. Later it became a mixing bowl for nomadic groups from Lemuria, Atlantis, and Yucatan. Eventually some migrated to the Midwest and set up another mysterious civilization.

Extracts from the Cayce Readings

"Before that we find the entity was in that land now known as Mu, or the vanished land of the Pacific, the Peaceful, during those periods when there were those banishments and preparations for the preserving, for they had known that the land must soon be broken up. The entity was among those that journeyed from Mu to what is now Oregon; and there still may be seen something of the worship as set up, in what was the development from that set up by the entity's associates, as the totem or family tree.

"In that experience the entity was in the same sex as at present, but among those that were the leaders; for then the women ruled, rather than men."   (Case # 630-2)

"Before that we find the entity was in that land now known as the American, during those periods when there were the changes that had brought about the sinking of Mu or Lemuria, or those peoples in the periods who had changed to what is now a portion of the Rocky Mountain area; Arizona, New Mexico, portions of Nevada and Utah. The entity then was among the princesses of the land that established there the teachings of the Law of One, from the activities of the land which had brought destructive forces through the separations from those things that made for the love of the individual for the gratification of selfish motives. Then the entity established what may be called the home life in that land, as each home became then as the castle or place of worship. . . . The name then was *Ouowu*."   (Case # 851-2)

"And when there became the hearsaying, yea, in those periods when there became an activity in which those portions of the land were discovered from what was left of Lemuria, or Mu—in what is now lower California, portions of the valleys of death—the entity journeyed there to see, to know. And during those experiences much was set up that may be of interest to the entity, that will be a part of the discoveries of nature or natural formations in what is now the Canyon Island. For this was the entity's place of the temple."   (Case # 1473–1)

"In the one before this we find in a strange land (Mu), now unknown in the world's experience; that lying westward from what is now southern California and Mexico. In this land the entity ruled as with an iron hand, for—from and through this land—many were the escapees from the various upheavals that occurred in those olden periods when there were the divisions of waters and the divisions of land, and dry land appeared. In this experience the entity lost, in the aggrandizement of selfish interest. In the name *Olu*."   (Case # 2669–1)

(A preponderance of vowels is noted in the names given—as in the modern languages of the Hawaiian and Polynesian peoples).

"Before that we find the entity was in that land now known as the American, during the periods when there were the sojournings of those from the land of Mu, or Lemuria. The entity was then among the first of those that were born in what is now a portion of Arizona and Utah, and among those that established the lands there for the building up or growing up of that civilization in these experiences; and was then in the name *Uuluoou*."   (Case # 691–1)

"The entity was in the land now known as Yucatan, when there were those establishings in the land from the Atlantean. The entity was in the temples, set as the recorder, in the name *Arsth*. In the experiences there were those periods of dissension with those in authority when there were the decisions of most of the peoples to join with the movement to what is now a portion of Arizona."   (Case # 5245–1)

"The entity was among those people who journeyed to the farther west or north and west from the Yucatan land; and the entity there (Arizona) was a priestess of the Children of the Law of One."   (Case # 1434–1)

"The entity was in the Atlantean land, during those periods when there was the breaking up and the journeying to the various lands. The entity was among those who came to what is now the Yucatan land, later journeying with many of those peoples to the south and west (of the U.S.)—or to portions of Arizona, as now known. Through the experience the entity was among those who made use of spiritual laws for material affectation; not so much in the abuse as in the negligence in supplying or in aiding others that were of the groups of 'things' to attain to a greater awareness."   (Case # 2576–1)

"The entity was in the Atlantean land, during those periods when there were the beginnings of the exodus owing to the destructive forces that had been begun by the Sons of Belial. The entity was among the princes of the land that made for the separating of those influences wherein there might be established the journeyings to other lands, with the keeping of records, with the permanent establishment of activities . . . in the Yucatan, in the Luzon, in what became the Inca, in the North American, and in what later became the land of the Mound Builders in Ohio . . . The entity then was not only one skilled in aircraft and in watercraft as an aviator and a navigator, but made great strides in keeping in touch with other lands through the forces of nature in the experience."
                                                      (Case # 1215–4)

CHAPTER EIGHT

WHO WERE THE MOUND BUILDERS?

From at least 3,000 years ago—perhaps 7,000—there lived in central United States a people who were remarkably skilled geometers. They had no written language, no wheels, lived always near the water, and apparently migrated along the Mississippi River and its tributaries. Strangest of all, they left behind them thousands of earthworks in the form of perfect squares, perfect circles, perfect squares within perfect circles, polygons, ellipses, sweeping arcs, and finely proportioned figures like the Great Serpent Mound near Peebles, Ohio.

Who were the Mound Builders? The answers have ranged from "A superior and distinct race" to nothing more than "Indians". Where they came from and how they developed no one really knows, although the consensus is that they likely were of Asiatic origin and somehow related to the Cliff Dwellers of the Southwest.

How they ran their society, fed it, led it, is another enigma. Little is known of the dynamics of their living except that they excelled in copper work, clay and bone-carving, built peculiar earthworks, and mysteriously passed on. Yet for centuries they ran a closely-knit society commanding a loyalty and discipline capable of building at least one structure many times as massive as the Great Pyramid of Egypt.

At Poverty Point, La., are the remains of a complex of mounds stretching for eleven miles. The intricate nature of the centrally planned community suggests that its designers came from Central America's Mayan culture, writes John Lear, Science Editor of the *Saturday Review* (Oct. 3, 1964). No longer married to the "Asiatic Bridge" theory, opinion has veered out of this well-worn rut to richer soil. "Today", writes Lear, "the weight of archaeological opinion favours the original notion that Poverty Point must have been a way-station for off-shoots of the Mayas or Aztecs en route up the Mississippi and Ohio river valleys."

The issue, however, has not yet been settled, for the earliest *Amerinds* were thought to be older than the Mayas, Aztecs and Incas and wholly distinct from them. Those of the valley areas, where they appear to have been superior and most heavily concentrated, defy identification with any known stock or people. Their highly developed and distinctive civilization make them unique, different from the modern American Indians found here by the white man.

It will be recalled that during the last Ice Age most of Eastern and Central United States was covered by glaciers. Some time after dry land appeared, around 10,000 B.C., the central portion became inhabitated, probably between 7000 and 3000 B.C. These people, the Mound Builders, were chiefly farmers rather than hunters. They were deeply religious, and their high morals and different dress—ornate and bejewelled—distinguish them. They believed in one God—the Magnificent Creator of Life. But they are best known for their many earthen mounds, the remains of which may be seen today chiefly in the South and Midwest.

These piles of earth range from a few feet in conical shape to rectangular ones 100 feet high covering 16 acres. There are perhaps 100,000 such mounds scattered over twenty states; from the Dakotas to Pennsylvania and from the Great Lakes to the Gulf of Mexico. Some are square and a few are flat-topped, but most are round or rectangular. The flat ones are believed to have supported temples, giving them a religious significance, but generally the mounds are presumed to have been primarily burial places, since only bones and artifacts have been found in the uncovered sites. The builders are known to have practised both cremation and burial of their dead.

Politically and economically, they seem to have led a communal life; there was apparently no private property or personal ownership of land. They therefore had some sort of community-held society.

The most famous site is the Serpent Mound in Adams County, Ohio. Of unknown date, it is 1,254 feet long, about 20 feet wide, and some 4–5 feet high, shaped like a coiled snake. Only a religious motive can explain its purpose. The mouth is open and appears to be about to swallow an egg, represented by a small, oval mound before it. *Kukulcan,* the Plumed Serpent god of Central Mexico, is brought to mind, as is the serpent in the Garden of Eden.

Evidently the Mound Builders carried on trade with one another over wide areas. Buried in the earth have been found pearls, conch shells from the Gulf, turquoise from the Southwest, grizzly bear teeth from the Rockies, mica from the Carolinas, copper ore from Lake Superior, and pottery designed like that found in Peru. Significantly, inscriptions recently discovered in Georgia depict a religious ceremony used by the Mayas and the ancient Jews of Palestine as recorded in the Book of Leviticus. Another late find, near Huntsville, Ala., indicates man lived there in 7000 B.C., an earlier date than previously supposed.

There were many tribes of Mound Builders, and their descendants gradually abandoned building the pyramids of earth. Their final disappearance is a mystery. Presumably they were overcome by other more warlike tribes and were eventually dispersed or absorbed. The consensus is that they did not disappear before the arrival of later Indians, or as a result of invasion. Rather, modern archaeologists hold to the view that they were the ancestors of the Indians of historic times.

The Iroquois, a confederacy of five large tribes or nations, appear to be related to them, as do the Algonquins of Canada. The Iroquois are noted for their superior agriculture and efficient statecraft. They too, as some other modern Indians, have legends of a great flood and the destruction of past worlds.

From the Cayce Records

A very few Life readings briefly state that many Atlanteans through their descendants struggled northward from Yucatan to Central United States, especially to the Mississippi Valley, Indiana, Kentucky and Ohio. With this major migration of uncertain date, they brought some of their former Atlantean religious tenets as well as the influences from the Mayan civilization in Yucatan, Honduras and Guatemala.

Later, joined by a group of people originally from Lemuria, they set up the culture that became known as the Mound Builders. They were farmers, raising wheat and grain, and cracking corn. Worshippers of nature, they paid homage to the sun and the rainfall in song and dance. The modern Iroquois Indians are their direct descendants.

Surprisingly, descendants of the Vikings, who arrived in Northeast U.S. in the eleventh and twelfth centuries A.D., came in contact with the Mound Builders and forged a close, friendly relationship with them.

Say the readings: "Before that the entity was in the land of the present nativity, during the early activities of a peoples that had been banished from Atlantis. The entity was among those of the second generation of Atlanteans who struggled northward from Yucatan, settling in what is now a portion of Kentucky, Indiana, Ohio; being among those of the earlier period known as Mound Builders.

"Then the entity was among those who supplied to the peoples the fruits of the soil, learning how to crack corn, wheat and grain, that it might be prepared into foods through cooking—though much in those periods was taken raw. And in the present, as the entity may learn, the raw foods will contribute much to the entity's welfare—the green as well as other foods." (Case # 35281–1)

Further we find, corroborating the belief of scholars in the relationship of the Mound Builders and the Iroquois, the following: "In the experience before this we find the entity was in the land of the present nativity. . . . The entity was then among the people, the Indians, of the Iroquois; those of noble birth, those that were the pure descendants of the Atlanteans, those that held to the ritualistic influences from nature itself." (Case # 1219–1)

Apparently the American colonies of the Northmen from Scandinavia endured longer than generally supposed, possibly for several generations, according to this reading: "The entity came into the Northeastern coast of this country, being among the descendants of the Norse peoples who first landed and settled there. Being strong physically, the entity gave much aid in establishing the forts and outposts of those who later joined with the people in the country south from there, who were known as the Mound Builders." (Case # 583–L–2)

Now we can turn to the vexing questions surrounding the Vikings and their sojourns in America, one of the most enigmatic stories of pre-Columbian history.

CHAPTER NINE

NORSEMEN IN NEW ENGLAND

The Goths of Norway and Sweden were probably the first white men to reach Eastern North America. Eric the Red, who was more popularly known as Eric the Lucky, was an early leader of the bold and brazen Vikings. The father of Leif Ericson, he sailed to Iceland in A.D. 970 and made a settlement there. Rumours of a great land to the west impelled him to sail in that direction, and in 980 he landed on the shores of Greenland, where he again started a new colony.

It was his son who first reached North America. Born in Iceland in 970, Leif Ericson grew up in Greenland in the tradition of a sea-going people who were vociferously proud of their courage. But his discovery of America in 1003 was quite by accident. Sailing from Norway under the auspices of the king, he was blown off course in a storm and landed on the east coast of the U.S. The exact location is disputed, but he reported finding wheat and grapes, and called the place "Vinland"—probably Cape Cod, Massachusetts.

Word of the new discovery spread, and other Norsemen were soon plying the coast of New England. Settlements were attempted but apparently they were short-lived. Presumably, these fair-haired, blue-eyed, "colourless" people were driven off by frightened, hostile Indians.

There is considerable evidence that Norsemen reached as far north and west as Minnesota. How they got here no one knows; probably via the Great Lakes, since being sailors it is unlikely they would travel that far by land.

A controversial discovery, known as the Beardmore find, was made in Ontario, Canada, on the north shore of Lake Superior. Uncovered were a broken Norse sword, an axe blade and parts of a shield. They are definitely of Viking origin. Yet the authenticity of the find was denied for years, and still is by some, on the ground that the implements were probably a hoax, although there was nothing to indicate this was the case. Why anyone would give up such valuable relics for a little private joke was not explained. Moreover, the Norsemen are known to have explored as far north as Hudson Bay.

The Director of the Danish National Museum later examined the pieces, as well as the famous Kensington Rune Stone, and declared there was no good reason to doubt the authenticity of either. To this day many authorities deny the validity of these two discoveries.

In 1898, a farmer in west-central Minnesota was grubbing his trees when he struck a large, oblong stone. Finally digging it up, he found a strange language inscribed on it. Scholars slowly recognized it as ancient Gothic, which contained only sixteen characters. Now known as the Kensington Rune Stone, it was disputed as a fraud. It read:

"We are 8 Goths (Swedes) and 22 Norwegians on an exploration journey from Vinland through the West. We had camp by a lake with two skerries (rocky islands) one day's journey north from this stone. We were out and fished one day. After we came home we found 10 of our men red with blood and dead. Ave Maria, save us from evil. We have 10 of our party by the sea to look after our ships (or ship), 14 days journey from this island. Year 1362."

In September 1967, Dr. O. G. Landsverk, America's leading Viking historian, declared the Kensington stone to be an authentic Norse cryptogram, and not a hoax. He places its date as May 7, 1244, based on the Norse Catholic Church calendar. The stone is on display in Alexandria, Minn. Never explained: Who would learn ancient Gothic, inscribe it, lug 230 pounds of stone to a remote farm field, bury it under tree roots and hope someone would discover it? The farmer? Just for kicks? More likely he died wishing he'd never heard of it!

Unfortunately, the Norsemen did leave little evidence of their sojourns in the United States. The Newport Tower of Rhode Island is, like the Kensington Stone, unacceptable to the sceptical conservatives. It is, writes one, "most likely a sixteenth-century English watchtower. The proof of mooring stones on the Atlantic seaboard, used to tie Viking ships, is flimsy at best. Some of the undoubtedly medieval Scandinavian weapons which turn up here and there, probably represent family heirlooms or collectors' items brought over not too long ago." These dubious explanations reveal nothing so much as the type of mind with which the student of antiquities has to deal.

"The lack of evidence", he concedes, "by no means weakened the likelihood of medieval landings, but it did reflect the rather incidental and haphazard nature of these enterprises which, for all we know, left no impact on pre-Columbian American developments."

There is no doubt that the Vikings reached and colonized the U.S., Iceland, and Greenland for perhaps 500 years. According to the Norse Saga narratives, a rich Greenlander with sixty others came to Vinland and set up a colony in 1007. It thrived for a time, but no more was heard of it. The disappearance of their colonies is a mystery. Possibly they were absorbed or slaughtered by the natives, or they simply died out. Reportedly, there are blue-eyed Mandan Indians of white blood in North Dakota, suggesting that the fair-skinned Northmen may indeed have tarried nearby. Lewis and Clark, in their expedition through the Northwest (1804–6), encountered friendly Indians there.

Remains of their stone structures and artifacts have been uncovered and identified beyond dispute, including a camp site in Newfoundland possibly belonging to Leif Ericson himself. Their many foreign journeys eventually reduced their numbers and strength at home, making them less adventuresome. Their exploration gradually came to an end around 1300. The last of the daring Vikings died out in Greenland in 1540, bringing an end to one of the most fascinating eras of early American history.

From the Cayce Records

According to seven Life readings in the files, Eric the Red, Leif Ericson, and other Norsemen made many trips across the Atlantic to the new lands of Iceland, Greenland, and America. They attempted to establish permanent settlements in Vinland, Massachusetts, and Rhode Island. None succeeded, but some of their people stayed there long enough to become rich and powerful by trading with friendly Indians. They returned to Norway wealthy persons, and somewhat heady.

"Before this we find the entity was during that period when Eric the Red made those voyages into the land of the entity's nativity in the present. The entity then was among those of that company who made the first attempts for the permanent settlement in that land known as the vineland, or coasts about Rhode Island and portions of the land lying north, or Massachusetts as called in the present.

"Then the entity was strong in body, in mind, and in the activities both on the land and the sea, and was in the name *Osolo Din.* Through the experience the entity gained and lost; gained in the aid given to the associates and companions in that particular experience of the life at that period; losing only when, with the material gains that came through the associations with the natives of the land, the entity acquired rather power, place and position. Hence, when there was the return to the land of birth in the experience, the entity not only rebelled but brought under submission those with whom he sailed to the land. This brought condemnation and hate in the experience during the latter portion of that sojourn." (Case # 438-1)

On one trip to America Eric the Red left his wife at home while other women were apparently making the long voyage. She was highly incensed, and the episode created a chasm between them that lasted for many years. Although a daring sailor, he was also a defiant individual, having bitter conflicts with the superiors under whom he served. Later in life he came to hate the sea because of his rigorous experiences with it.

But in America, he once travelled as far as west-central Minnesota, and some of his men remained there to live the rest of their lives among the Indians. This is one of the reasons why Lewis and Clark expeditions through the area met no resistance from the Indians there. Some Vikings reached as far west as Montana. "Before this the entity was in the Norse land, among those who journeyed into the greater western portion or near to the central portion of Minnesota in the present land of nativity, when Eric the Red was among those active there. The entity then, as *Olsen-Olsen,* became among those who journeyed there and remained to become a part of those peoples in that land. Thus were the northwestern lands made available when Clark made the expedition there, so that there were not the activities against those peoples at the time. Thus may the entity use itself as a peacemaker among those of various groups, tribes, nations or countries." (Case # 3651–1)

Leif Ericson, with *Olaf* and *Olensen,* landed at Martha's Land and Vinland, in Connecticut and Massachusetts. On another trip, Ericson and his crew founded a colony near what is now Providence, Rhode Island. Others also made numerous voyages to Newfoundland and Nova Scotia. But Vinland was one of the first settlements, and although later abandoned, a few chose to remain there, developing a "spiritual" brotherhood with the natives and discovering a "short way across New York State".

Interestingly, Eric the Red has reincarnated in the earth. "Before this the entity was in the Norse land, among those who were the daring, as the sailors; and the entity was Eric, as called through that experience; journeying to or settling in the land of its present nativity. Yet with the experiences through the latter portion of its sojourn, and the activities from which it returned in the period or interim, the entity in the present—as indicated—is averse to water, waterways, water carriers.

"Hence the daring now is exhibited more in the air, or in ships of the air—arising from another sojourn. . . . In that experience the entity gained, the entity lost; for there were periods of defiance of not only its associates and companions but of its home life, and the superiors under which the entity acted or laboured." (Case # 2157–1)

Thus ends the story, unhappily, of the Norsemen in America according to the Cayce files.

We have reviewed the course of human events up to the fringes of modern history. The Cayce records contain readings on practically every period of American life and times. There are reincarnations of soul entities from the Revolutionary War, witchcraft in New England, pioneer days in the Midwest, the Civil War, opening of the West, World Wars I and II.

Although many of these discourses make fascinating

reading and reveal the lives of some fabulous if not famous or altogether discreet characters, they add but little of importance to what is already known. We will therefore turn our attention to the more crucial and complex problems existing in America today and tomorrow. For the fabric of the present and future is closely interwoven and dependent upon the threads of the past.

PART THREE

1998 AND BEYOND

CHAPTER TEN

CRISIS IN MODERN AMERICA

Edgar Cayce had a great deal to say about the future of the United States. As the wheels of history continue to turn, mankind is rapidly approaching a new cycle. We are now well into the transition period to the "new dispensation"—the "time and times and half times are at an end. The righteous shall inherit the earth," say the readings.

But it will not be easy; indeed it will be a period of discord, strife and turbulence that will try men's souls, and "many will fall away". Yet we need to remember that from the grinding, grating friction within the oyster comes the pearl. There is no growth without adversity. History, which often repeats itself, reveals the truth that for every force there is a counter-force, for every negative there is a positive. This is part of the evolutionary process of man's long tenure in the earth.

That a new age is to be born in the year 1998 was predicted in the Cayce readings in the 1930's. Since then other sources have named approximately the same date. Even such an orthodox body as the American Academy of Arts and Science has sponsored a commission to study the coming state of Western society by the year 2000, because that year is expected to usher in another great "system break". The signposts are out at every turn of the road.

"The West—and particularly the U.S.—is expected to achieve a state in which economically we shall have it made," writes Henry Winthrop, a professor of social sciences. "It is widely believed that by the year 2000, there will be plenty for all, made possible by automation, computers and other major technological advances which are now foreseen."

He does not discuss the enormous yet delicate problem of the system and method of distribution—the real question —but does add that there will be more time and interest in "leisure, education, culture, the widening of the horizons of consciousness and the quest for deep emotional and religious experiences." This includes pursuit of the arts, sciences, and mathematics; new forms of architecture and community planning, experiments with new ideas in psychological sensitivity, and a more experimental attitude towards new social institutions.

Utopian, some may say. Perhaps. But entirely possible and certainly desirable. Already the new vision has produced a generation gap—an information gap, in fact—between the young and not so young. An artificial wedge has been driven between the two. We should not make the tragic mistake of selling short the new generation, but ask, Will the older generation rise to the occasion? Or will it insist that its materialistic values and attitudes are good for all time, and that the youth of today are just a bunch of impractical, immature, idealistic students? Rather, we should ask if we have lived up to our own ideals, and examine our own inconsistencies.

However mistaken its views on sex and drugs, the youth are rebelling because they feel they have been deceived by a hypocritical society. Home and church, to give just one example, taught them to respect property and the rights of others. When they grow up and go into the military, they're taught how to destroy property and kill people. So they become conscientious objectors and burn their draft cards. Moreover, they have a feeling of brotherhood, an *esprit de corps* lacking in the recent past. They're the first generation that has had time to think.

There are, of course, other areas of conflict ahead of us that must be resolved before the New Age can come into being. The price of our poverty is too high. As Gunnar Myrdal so aptly put it: "America cannot afford to remain the one among the rich countries which has the highest rate of unemployment, which has the worst and biggest slums, which is least generous in giving economic security to its old people, its children, its sick and its invalids."

One of the bitter paradoxes of our age is that amidst so much wealth of the few there is so much poverty among the many. We need not only to live and let live for moral and ethical reasons, there are concrete, practical reasons why we should do so. Continuing higher rates of violence, crime, fraud, tax loopholes, deception, inflation, price-rigging mark the state of moral decay of an opulent society in mad pursuit of the dollar. The decline of American morality is an effect, not a cause. The many ills besetting our society are obvious enough; the underlying reasons are more subtle.

What can one expect when there is corruption and deception in high places—the Government, the CIA, big business, the military-industrial-congressional complex. Do we have a house of cards built on sand? Are the merits of their position so weak that they must lie? Would the truth be self-condemning? More broadly, has the older generation sold its soul for pieces of silver?

The Pentagon, originally a plane figure of five sides, is now a complex with many angles; the country used to be on the gold standard, now it's on the Brass. And the CIA, FBI, and Army Intelligence have become the Departments of Offence. Unfortunately, as former General Maxwell Taylor once testified before a Congressional committee, the moral factor is not an issue in government decisions.

The Cold War is over economic and social issues, not military ones; international markets, natural resources, hegemony over under-developed countries, social security for the plain people. Communism is a challenge, not a threat. The real question is, can capitalism compete with socialism? Or must it resort to military means?

Twice during World War I Cayce was called secretly to Washington and Woodrow Wilson's fourteen points in the peace treaty and his plan for the League of Nations reveal much of the readings' philosophy. No record of what transpired exists today, but a later reading indicated that Wilson was a far more spiritual-minded man than was generally recognized. "The Christ spirit sat at the peace table," Cayce said. Biographies of Wilson support what the readings had to say. The vicious opposition of the Sons of Belial put Wilson in his grave, emasculated the 14 points, and killed the League of Nations. Karma! The Allies paid the price in World War II.

Since then, a new, low standard has been set for the nation, and the residue is seeping down to the people. Yet the System somehow demands a higher morality from the public than it itself is willing to uphold. This is a fallacy and today impossible.

Back of it all is the greed of a few. It is profitable to produce armaments, films of sex and violence, pornographic "literature"; it is profitable to sell worthless land and stocks, to rig prices and defraud the public in a thousand different ways. It is all done in the search for profits, power and prestige by the few—and for the haunting, gnawing guarantee of security by the many. In brief, the wolves are turned loose on the rabbits—the innocent, the unsuspecting, the uneducated—and some wonder why the rabbits are running berserk! The system is an open range.

The honest, small, business man is slowly becoming, like the family farmer, extinct. Independence and integrity have little chance of survival against powerful, unscrupulous, absentee ownership. And absentee ownership is one of the primary causes of our deteriorating social structure.

Suppose the direct, private, profit motive were absent. Suppose every productive person's security in old age were guaranteed. Are these reasons the Incas and others had such low rates of crime and poverty? We need to ask ourselves some hard questions. Is the capitalist system based on the survival of the fittest? Is it of the law of the jungle? A philosophy of every man for himself, pitting man against man? Does it appeal to man's most gross instincts? Does it invite him to deceive, to cheat, to rob in order to sustain himself and ensure security?

A great deal needs to be done to set the corporate house aright. Capitalism is committing suicide. The question is, can it, or will it reform through either self-discipline or compulsory regulation? It is possible but not probable that private enterprise will have the necessary vision to transform itself to better serve the common good. There are few indications that it will do so.

The university students understand all this better than their elders. They know the score and understand the game. Dr. Calvin H. Plimpton, President of Amherst College, succinctly spelled out the campus view in a letter to President Nixon: "We believe that we must speak out to make clear that much of the turmoil among young people and among those who are dedicated to humane and reasoned changes will continue. It will continue until you and the other political leaders of our country address more effectively, massively, and persistently the major social and foreign problems of our society. Part of this turmoil in universities derives from the distance separating the American dream from the American reality."

After pointing out the "shoddiness of many aspects of our society", and the absence of a sense of purpose, Dr. Plimpton went on: ". . . until political leadership addresses itself to the major problems of our society—the huge expenditure of national resources for military purposes, the inequities practised by the present draft system, the critical needs of America's 23 million poor, the unequal division of our life on racial issues—until this happens, the concern and energy of those who know the need for change will seek outlets for their frustration."

The "Yippies", the young intellectuals of the Left, and the "Hippies" use whatever methods are at hand to demonstrate their disenchantment with the status quo. A few simply reject and opt-out of the entire system. Others, like the "Bible Hippies", take an almost puritanical view of our preoccupation with prurient things. Many believe the church has lost its way and become irrelevant in combating the crucial problems of the day. They have a folk song that goes, "The Lord is not impressed with worldly success." Some radicals no longer believe the capitalist parties can be reformed to become responsive to and representative of the people. Almost all are perceptive enough and astute enough to see through the glittering, polished veneer of a success-intoxicated culture. We do not have to condone everything they do or say in order to understand this.

Unfortunately, the Empire Builders have cried Wolf so often through popular media about the horrors of slavery under godless communism, that few any longer listen. Now that a tacit understanding with the Soviets is imminent, the Establishment must try to undo its own propaganda—no small task considering the years devoted to the binding of men's minds. "Freedom of the press" has been interpreted as licence to take liberties with the truth. The harbingers of hate have displayed more interest in forming public opinion than in informing the public. Craftsmen in the art of political science fiction, some are now rebelling against the present fascist trend in America.

And there are mountainous problems on the international scene crying for solution. Several years ago this writer said (*The Churchman* magazine, June 1962), after a trip abroad: "I am one of those Americans who believes there must eventually be a meeting ground between the two most powerful nations in history. We are all part of the Brotherhood of Man and the Fatherhood of God. It behooves us therefore, to row together rather than separately against the stream of adversity, for there is enough of that already without manufacturing more between each other.

"We live in trying times. The underdeveloped peoples of the world are seeking and demanding their rightful place in the sun. They want their country for themselves; no one can safely hold back the tide of change. Indeed, the 'haves' are morally obligated to share their abundance with the 'have-nots'—not in the weapons of destruction, which have no intrinsic value and serve only to create suspicion and tension—but in the necessities of life; food, factories, schools, dams, hospitals. It is catastrophic that the two nations most suited to do this are at odds over how it should be done and who should do it . . .

"We are losing the cold war, the battle for the minds of men. There are certain elements in powerful positions who, when they recognize this, might not hesitate to turn it into a hot one. Only the weight of public opinion would stand in the way. Yet the critical condition in which we find ourselves is a direct result of our own complacency. We are reaping just what we have sown in our indifference toward national and international problems." Karma!

But the younger generation is not so complacent. They care. They are serious. And they don't like many of the things they've inherited. Extremists all, they intend to change things. The handwriting is already on the wall for those who can read it.

One might well ask, who are these amazing people, and what do they want? In order to understand, appreciate, perhaps participate in the passing parade—truly the greatest show on earth—we need to explore at some length the coming New Order and how it is to be reached.

The first allusions to the new generation appear in Cayce readings for people born around 1917–20. Others came along later, but almost all were Atlanteans reincarnating in the earth in large numbers for a purpose. Presumably they're still coming in. It appears that this influx of experienced, developed souls—aggressive as well as progressive —represents group or nation karma. The present age would offer the first opportunity since the fall of Atlantis to meet certain problems under similar circumstances.

They bring a new standard of ethics, and they are making their presence felt in many parts of the world. Their physical vigour and high mentality together with their past history and store of unconscious knowledge will reshape societies throughout the earth. In some countries they have already attempted to do so, and have sometimes in part succeeded. The youth of South Korea were not the first of the new breed to depose a despotic ruler, Syngman Rhee, in 1960; Castro did it in 1958.

The transition "will begin in those periods in 1958 to 1998," state the readings. "When this period has been accomplished, then the New Era, the New Age, is to begin. Will you have a part in it, or will you let it pass by, and merely be a hangeron . . ." (Case # 364 series)

In the beginning, man was commanded to multiply and subdue the earth—not to subtract, divide and subdue one another. *Self*. That is the root cause of the dissensions today; the differences of opinions, the classes, the castes; and of social, economic, political systems, Cayce said. "America has lost its ideal."

It is a small world, and growing smaller by the day. The population expansion, over which we hear such cries of anguish and doom, may well be a blessing in disguise. Surely it is by design, not by accident. It is forcing to the forefront economic and social issues that have been neglected for centuries, and bringing about changes undreamed of even a generation ago.

"With the advent of the closeness of worlds coming into being, so that man upon the other side of earth is as much the neighbour as the man next door, more and more have been the turmoils that have arisen in the attempt of individual leaders of groups to induce, force or compel one portion of the world to think as the other; or the other group to dwell together as brethren with one bond of sympathy, or one standard for all.

"With the present conditions then that exist—these have all come to that place in the development of the human family where there must be a reckoning, a point upon which all may agree, that of all this turmoil that has arisen from the social life, racial differences, the outlook upon the relationships of man to the Creative Forces or his God, and his relationships one with another, must come to some common basis upon which all may agree." (Case # 3976 series; 1932)

"Man's answer to everything has been power—power of money, power of position, power of wealth, power of this, that or the other. This has never been God's way, will never be God's way." And the true test of leadership is that men must "choose either to serve those in high places or to serve mankind as a whole." (Case # 364 series)

The following is an eloquent example of group karma, of compensatory reaction to a previous action. In 1932, Cayce said: "Europe is as a house broken up. Some years ago there was the experience of a mighty peoples being overridden for the gratification and satisfaction of a few, irrespective of others' rights. That peoples are going through the experience of being born again, and are the thorn in the flesh to many a political and financial nation in Europe, in the world . . ." (Case # 364 series)

A question revealed that the Russians were the people reincarnating, evidently those who had suffered under the czars.

"There is no activity in the experience of man that has not its inception or purpose in the spirit of those injunctions (of love, fairness) but what must fail unless it is founded in the spirit of truth." For "God is not mocked, and whatsoever a man, a country, a nation sows, that it must reap." For every action, there is a reaction, for every cause, an effect.

"As is understood by many, in the earth manifestation and the cycle of time, much repeats itself; and those in authority, in high and low places, have the opportunity for individual expression." And he added, "There is nothing new under the sun. What is has been, and will be again." (Case # 1149–10)

"The ideals, the purposes that called the (American) nation into being are well," he said in 1939. "It might be answered by saying that there needs to be on the part of each man, each woman, the adhering to those principles that caused the formulating of the American thought."

(Case # 1149–7½) Apparently this refers to the Declaration of Independence, the Constitution and the Bill of Rights. We have since drifted so far Right that they could not pass the Congress today.

Someone asked the sleeping psychic about the future of religion in the U.S. "That depends upon the activities of too many individuals for this to be prognosticated at the present time; for changes are coming, this may be sure—an evolution, or revolution in the ideas of religious thought. The basis of it for the world will eventually come out of Russia; not communism, NO! But rather that which is the basis of the same, as the Christ taught—His kind of communism!" (Case # 425–5).

We cannot be certain of the full meaning here. The Essenes, who reared and tutored the youth Jesus, lived communally; not only the real property but even the personal property was owned by the group as a whole. Acts 2:44 and 4:32 speak of all things being held in common. Yet "the basis of the same" could be the spirit of fraternity motivating a closer union of individuals in a group.

Americans do not want and are not spiritually prepared for communism in any form. Yet the cooperative impulse in man is as great or greater than the competitive one. Competition has its place, but in survival it is brutal, impoverishing and out of place.

In 1934, Cayce said, "If there is not the acceptance in America of the closer brotherhood of man, the love of the neighbour as self, civilization must wend its way westward —and again must Mongolia, must a hated people, be raised." He made clear the interdependence of men and nations when he added, "There has arisen, and there is arising in the affairs and experiences of man everywhere the necessity of there being not so much the consideration of a land as of all lands as a unit." (Case # 3976 series) The truth of this is now self-evident.

The Cayce readings throughout place the final burden on the individual. "Let each know that it is a harp upon which the breath of God would play . . . as seekers after divine guidance be uplifted; and thus may ye hasten the day when war will be no more." He was not above cracking the whip on occasion. Regarding a question on the "protection of our democracy", Cayce answered, "Raise not democracy nor any other name above the brotherhood of man, the Fatherhood of God!" He once admonished, "Ye cannot pray *peace, peace,* when there is no peace in thine own heart and soul!"

Cayce predicted the present crisis in America three decades ago, and he named the basic cause of it. In June 1943, the sleeping prophet said: "As for this own land, more turmoils will be in and following peace—not immediate—than there are in the present. These will be turmoils from within: Lack of godliness in the hearts of some of those who direct the affairs of groups." He could not have been more accurate.

"It is understood, comprehended by some that a new order of conditions is to arise," he said in 1938, "that there must be a purging in high places as well as low; that there must be the greater consideration of the individual, each soul being his brother's keeper. There will then come about those circumstances in the political, the economic, the social relationships where there will be a leveling—or a greater comprehension of this need." (Case # 1149 series)

The purging of those in low places has never been much of a problem—they're accustomed to it. Purging those in high places is not so easy; they are accustomed to doing the purging.

What should be our attitude toward the Negro, someone asked. "He is thy brother! They that produced, they that brought servitude without thought or purpose have created that which they must meet within their own principles, their own selves. These should be taken in the attitude of their own individual fitness, as in every other form of association. For He hath made of one blood the nations of the earth." (Case # 1149 series)

Obviously a karmic situation, we now find ourselves faced with an I.O.U. of 300 years standing. It will likely require a couple generations of higher education and economic equality to alleviate the years of oppression. The black man is largely the product of the white South, a fact of which no one boasts, some will admit, and few are willing to accept the responsibility for. Basically a spiritual people, and not without talent, what they most need is opportunity, a commodity that has always been in short sup-

ply. The militant blacks of today are the former slave hold-
ers of earlier America, says Cayce. They will not tolerate
oppression.

"There cannot be one measuring rod for the labourer,"
Cayce said in 1938, "and another for the man behind the
money changers. All are equal . . . Though there may
come those periods when there will be great stress, as
brother rises against brother, as group or sect or race rises
against one another . . . the levelling must eventually
come . . . And then there should be, there will be, those
rising to power who are able to meet the needs (of the
times)." (Case # 1149 series)

The levelling is now at hand, and hopefully there are
men of vision and principle emerging to show the way by
reform and peaceful evolution. But the enormity of the
problems is almost overwhelming. It may already be too
late.

"Every phase of human experience and human relationship must be taken into consideration. If those in position
to give of their means, their wealth, their education, *do not*
take these things into consideration, there must be that
levelling that will come. For unless the needs are considered there must eventually come a revolution in this country—and there will be a dividing of the sections as one
against another. For these are the levelling means and
manners to which men resort when there is plenty in some
areas and lack of sustenance in the life of others. These are
the sources from which such things as crime, riots, and
every nature of disturbance arise—in that those who are
in authority are not considering every level, every phase of
human activity and human experience." (Case # 1149
series)

Blunt words prophetically spoken. And as so often is the
case, they deal with root causes, not just effects or by-
products. Cayce once made a perplexing remark difficult to
place in context. He said, "When the true position of some
becomes known, consternation will prevail among the
people." We can therefore expect some kind of exposure or
voluntary disclosure that will shock the nation.

"Those in power must know that they are their brother's
keeper, and give expression to that which has been indicated in, 'Thou shalt love the Lord with all thy heart and

mind and body, and thy neighbour as thyself'. This rule
must be applied. It is true that in some of those factions in
Russia this is an attempt; yet there *are* those who have
applied and do apply the same in not only the economic
life but attempt to do the same in the mental and spiritual
life. And this brings hardship where it should not be."

Evidently the latter comment is a reference to the re-
strictions on speech and religion so prevalent under Stalin
in 1938, the year of the reading. Man should be his
brother's keeper, but that doesn't mean he owns his soul.

"From the conditions in other lands," Cayce went on,
"America must take warning. For to whom does the
wealth belong? To whom do the possibilities of the land
belong? Does it belong to those who have inherited it, to
those who have been given the position of power? Or to
those who have by their labour, by the sweat of their brow
produced same? (Emphasis E. C's in all cases).

"Not that all would be held in common, as in the communistic idea, save as to keep the balance, to keep that
oneness, to keep that association of ideas and activity . . .
for all . . . So long as there are disputes among labour,
capital need not fear. When labour becomes a *united*
effort, capital may fear . . . in the same principle that he
that labours may eat, he that labours not may not eat.
These are principles; and to be sure, capital labours as well
as he that worketh with the hands. But *not* to the detriment
of, but to the united effort of all . . ."

Labour has never been truly united, except on paper.
The AFL-CIO coalition merely pasted over the cracks.
George Meany, representing the conservative element, and
Walter Reuther the liberal movement, were long at odds.
Which wing will win is almost a foregone conclusion, but
how and when the unions decide to join their unions will
be interesting to see. Only 22 per cent of the U.S. labour
force is organized. The warning to capital is clear enough;
it needs to become more socially conscious and responsible.
One dilemma is job opportunities, with retirement still at
age 65.

"Ye are to have turmoils, ye are to have strifes between
capital and labour. Ye are to have a division in thine own
land before there is the second of the Presidents that next
will not live through his office—a mob rule!" And we need

to prepare ourselves "for the nation coming into existence". (Case # 1149 series)

Here we have an enigma. From the point of view that Franklin Roosevelt lived through three and a fraction offices, John Kennedy would be the first since this reading (1939) to "not live through his office", the first term of his office. Some students of the Cayce records believe however, that Kennedy's assassination was the second, although there was no real "division in the land" then between capital and labour and hardly a "mob rule" in the context of the readings and the full meanings of those terms. It would appear that perhaps these events still lie ahead of us, if such a view is indeed a valid one. Or Cayce may simply be wrong.

"That such is, and is to be a part of the experience of America is because of unbelief!" And later he added in the same discourse, "Unless there is, then, a more universal oneness of purpose on the part of all, this will one day bring here in America—revolution!"

The need is great; the time is short. The warning is directed to all, and especially to "those who control or direct the investing of capital". For, "Those who are hungry care not as to the source of strength or power until there is the fulfilling of that desired." (Case # 1149 series)

Cayce never set any date, but in 1940 he gave some indications. "When many of the isles of the sea, many of the lands have come under the subjugation of those who fear not man nor the devil, but rather would associate with that in which they may proclaim *might* and power as being right . . . then shall thine own land see the blood flow as in those periods when brother fought against brother."

Does this refer to the 2,000 South Pacific islands the U.S. acquired control of after World War II, and certain Latin American and Asian lands? If it does, the time is short indeed.

Equally startling is this comment made on the Soviet Union in 1933. "On Russia's religious development will come the greater hope of the world. Then that one, or group, that is closer in its relationships may fare the better in the gradual changes and the final settlement of conditions as to the rule of the world." (Case # 364–Sa3)

This statement was not clarified until 1944. "In Russia

there comes the hope of the world, not as that sometimes termed the communistic, the Bolshevistic; no. But freedom, freedom in that each man will live for his fellow man! The principle has been born. It will take years for it to be crystallized, but out of Russia comes again the hope of the world. Guided by what? That friendship with the nation that hath even set on its present monetary unit, In God we Trust!" And later we find, ". . . for tomorrow China will awake".

China did awake, and threw off the burden of a shortsighted capitalism seemingly bent on its own destruction. Man's greed is greater than his wisdom. Unfortunately, the people of China became subjected to another form of autocracy. Hopefully, it too is now evolving.

For the past several years the U.S. and the U.S.S.R. have been working toward a détente. That they will move even closer together is no longer surprising. Fear is the new enemy. The motivation may be fear or peace, but the end result will be the same: co-existence on a new, broader plane. The Soviet Union is now moving slowly to the Right; the U.S. has since the 1930's been shifting to the Left, if in a low gear. Both will likely borrow the best from each other to fit their own particular needs. Economic systems, as distinct from political systems, have a way of crossing barriers. They also have a way of making devils out of saints.

Today we stand at the edge of a volcano. The Juggernaut—the big money interests, the military-industrial-congressional complex—is confronted with a generation it does not understand nor know how to cope with. The young are not buying the myths, slogans and clichés that have so successfully glossed over realities in the past. Daily the lines are being drawn; the camps are forming; the issues are waiting to be joined. The growing voice of discord is making itself heard in many quarters. The question is, do the Empire Builders get the message?

The Sons of Belial are back. In Atlantis they 'won', and brought destruction upon themselves. Is the ancient conflict between the Children of the Law of One and the Sons of Belial being repeated? If so, it will present us with a bold challenge and a magnificent opportunity that will try men's souls. But the situation may yet be saved. Only drastic reform will suffice. It is not too late, but it is very nearly so.

Unhappily, America's troubles will be compounded in other areas; crises will arise besides those of a political, social, and economic nature. The period of 1958 to 1998 will, according to the Cayce records, bring radical changes in the geography of the Western Hemisphere, and especially that of North America. The face of the U.S. will change its appearance.

"Study of approximately fifty Edgar Cayce readings that describe past geologic events indicates that the information given in the readings is internally logical and consistent", reports one professional geologist with a Ph.D. degree, who understandably prefers to remain anonymous. Yet, as to be expected, "Only a few. . . . agree closely with current scientific *facts*; a number of them stand in contrast to present *concepts* of earth history."

Then he adds: "The many catastrophic events that are predicted for this period are out of harmony with the standard geological concept of uniformitarianism (i.e., gradual changes rather than sudden ones). It is of interest, however, that certain events predicted in the readings, for the period 1926 to 1958, occurred as prophesied. Examples are an earthquake in California on October 22, 1926; violent wind storms on the 15th and 20th of October, 1926; and the general location of strong earthquakes in California between 1926 and 1950."

In 1934, Cayce predicted: "The earth will be broken up in many places. The early portion ('58 to '98) will see a change in the physical aspect of the west coast of America. There will be open waters to appear in the northern portions of Greenland. There will be new lands seen off the Caribbean Sea, and dry land will appear. . . . South America shall be shaken from the uppermost portion to the end, and in the Antarctic off Tierra Del Fuego, land, and a strait with rushing waters." (Case # 3976–15)

In 1959, the U.S. Coast and Geodetic Survey reported that a large quake had taken place where earthquakes have never occurred before—in the northern Magellan Strait near the tip of South America. Chile, the west coasts of California and Alaska are experiencing quakes and tremors. Are these forerunners of events to come?

"Many portions of the east coast will be disturbed, as well as many portions of the west coast, as well as the central portion of the United States. In the next few years lands will appear in the Atlantic as well as in the Pacific. And what is the coast line now of many a land will be the bed of the ocean. Even many of the battlefields of the present (1941) will be in the ocean, will be the seas, the bays, the lands over which the new order will carry on their trade as one with another.

"Portions of the now east coast of New York, or New York City itself, will in the main disappear. This will be another generation, though, here; while the southern portions of Carolina, Georgia, these will disappear. This will be much sooner." (Case # 1151–11).

There has been increased seismic activity in eastern Canada, New England, and New York in recent years, for earthquakes are not restricted to recognized zones. At least one seismologist, L. Don Leet of Harvard, is concerned that a big quake may very well hit some unpredictable eastern seaboard spot before the century is over. Information on the Carolinas and Georgia is scanty, but the Coast and Geodetic Survey in 1959 reported that the land surface about Savannah subsided as much as four inches since 1933.

"The waters of the lakes (Great Lakes) will empty into the Gulf (of Mexico), rather than the waterway over which such discussions have been recently made (St. Lawrence Seaway)." The areas of much of Ohio, Indiana, Illinois will be safe, however.

Another "shifting of the poles", as Cayce once suggested, could indeed cause the Great Lakes to drain to the Mississippi Valley, perhaps creating a river matching the Nile or the Amazon. The Lakes are known to be tilting southwestwardly gradually—at a rate of five inches per hundred miles per century at present. "It would be well if the waterway were prepared," he said, "but not for that purpose for which it is at present being considered." A clear reference to the St. Lawrence Seaway, it has since been built.

"All over the country we will find many physical

changes of both a minor or major degree. The greater change, as we will find, will be the North Atlantic Seaboard. Watch New York, Connecticut, and the like" (Case # 311–8). Manhattan Island will be hardest hit, and Norfolk, Va., he predicted, will become the main seaport. In fact, it now leads the nation in tonnage handled.

"Los Angeles, San Francisco—most all of these will be among those that will be destroyed before New York, even." An indication of the time is given in the following: "If there are the greater activities in the Vesuvius, or Pelee, then the southern coast of California—and the areas between Salt Lake and the southern portions of Nevada—may expect, within the three months following same, an inundation by the earthquakes" (Case # 270–35). He also said to watch Mt. Etna, and recent volcanic action has been reported there.

California sits astride the great San Andreas land fault, a fracture 15 miles deep and 2,000 miles long. Professor Hugo Benioff of the Institute of Technology, and probably the world's leading authority on earthquakes, has stated that the city of Los Angeles could be devastated any day, a probability long recognized. Considering the large numbers of people who have been attracted to California in recent years, one can only wonder what the karmic significance might be, a subject we will discuss in a later chapter.

"Lands will appear in the Atlantic as well as the Pacific." This sounds pretty far out, until we recall that as recently as November 1963, a new island was suddenly created by volcanic eruption off the coast of Iceland. Named *Surtsey*, it rose overnight to a height of 30 feet, and is still there.

"Poseidia will be among the first portions of Atlantis to rise again," said Cayce. "Expect it in sixty-eight and sixty-nine. Not so far away!" Poseidia was the most important Atlantean island after the first cataclysm, containing the leading port city of the same name. It was located in the area of the Bahama Islands. Dr. Manson Valentine's discovery of temple-like structures there in 1968, 69, 70 indicates the accuracy of Cayce's prophecy.

"As time draws nigh when changes are to come about, there may be the opening of those three places where the

records (of the Atlanteans) are one, to those that are the
initiates in the knowledge of the One God: The temple
(near Bimini) will rise again; also there will be the opening
of the temple of records in Egypt; and those records that
were put into the heart of the Atlantean land may also be
found there. The records are one." (Case # 5750–1)

But Cayce's fallibility is disclosed when he predicted
land changes in Alabama in 1936–38. None occurred.

The question naturally arises: Why are all these turmoils
and eruptions taking place now, in the United States, at
this particular period of history? Why indeed should they
happen at all? The Cayce files reveal some astonishing reasons, indicating it is the sin of man. In answer to a question
about sun spots, he once said:

"As the sun has been set as the ruler of this solar system,
does it not appear to be reasonable that it has an effect
upon the inhabitants of the earth as well as upon plant and
mineral life in the earth? . . . As the sun is made to shed
light and heat upon God's children in the earth, it is then
of that composition of which man is made, or of that
termed the earth; yet as ye have seen and know, there is
solid matter, there is liquid, there is vapour. All are one in
their various stages of activity for what? Man—*Godly
man!* Yet when these (men) become as in defiance to that
light which was commanded to march, to show forth the
Lord's glory, His beauty, His mercy, His hope—yea, His
patience—do ye wonder then that there becomes reflected
upon even the face of the sun those turmoils and strifes that
have been and are the sin of man?" (Case # 5757–1)

If this is true, the sun has a sensitivity never before sus-
pected. Cayce explained it this way: "How does anger,
jealousy, hate, animosity effect thee? Much as that confusion which is caused upon the earth by that which appears as a sun spot. The disruption of communications of
all natures between men is what? Remember the story, the
allegory if ye choose to call it such, of the Tower of Babel."
He then concludes with this admonishment: "For, as ye do
it unto the least, ye do it unto the Maker—even as to the
sun which reflects those turmoils that arise with thee, even
as the earthquakes, even as wars and hates, even as the influences in thy life day by day. Then, what are the sun
spots? A natural consequence of that turmoil which the

sons of God in the earth reflect upon same." (Case # 5757–1)

On October 30, 1968, the Louisville, Ky., *Courier-Journal* carried the following Associated Press story: "Storms on the face of the sun caused wide-ranging interference with short-wave radio communications yesterday. . . . Causing the activity is a cluster of solar flares, areas of intensified magnetic activity within specific regions of the sun's magnetic field. . . . It is believed the increased activity is associated with the 'year of the angry sun' expected in 1969. Next year is expected to mark the stormy peak of the current 11-year cycle of solar activity."

On August 10, 1969, an Orbiting Solar Observatory, OSO 6, was launched to produce, said AP, "the best information yet about solar radiation storms that disrupt radio communications on earth and are a potential danger to astronauts flying in deep space." Scientists are particularly interested in high-energy rays that spawn solar flares —violent thermonuclear eruptions on the sun's surface that send radiation storms through space affecting the northern lights and possibly this planet's weather, wildlife, even earthquakes.

Thus the law of action and reaction—karma—may indeed be universal. Cayce insisted again and again that past, present, and future strifes, disturbances, upheavals are the result of man's disobedience. If true, the Biblical passage, "Be not deceived, for God is not mocked," takes on new meaning. The law of cause and effect may be more far-reaching than heretofore thought possible.

CHAPTER ELEVEN

THE COMING NEW ORDER

A new era of great expectations is upon us. The *status quo* is obviously no longer good enough, nor will it suffice to meet the challenges of the times ahead of us. But by whatever route the new age is attained, what can we expect in 1998?

Orthodox communism in practice is becoming obsolete because of its inequities. Socialism, while having some merit, can lead to the bureaucracy and oppressiveness of a centralized, authoritarian, top-heavy government. Myopic capitalism is going blind, it apparently cannot read the handwriting on the wall.

"In America, in the political forces," Cayce said, "we see a restabilization of the powers of the peoples in their own hands—a breaking up of the rings, the cliques in many places" (Case # 3876 series). To the Big Money boys, that statement is heresy or worse, contrary to their view of power from the top down, not from the bottom up.

"Remember that those principles inculcated in the Declaration (of Independence) are eternal, and in them lies the hope of the world (politically). All men must recognize them if they are to remain together as brethren; in that they all need not be of one mind, but they must all be of one purpose, one hope . . .", based on equality, fraternity, understanding. (Case # 5053–L1)

The principle of the Brotherhood of man and the Fatherhood of God will eventually prevail, and "all are to work in unison for the good of all," in a "cooperative, coordinating" society. But there is need for "more world-thinking" and less nationalism, and an international currency or "international stabilization of exchange values," Cayce said. The urgency here is now obvious. Our gold reserves and balance of payments are in serious trouble; collapse of the French franc, English pound, or the dollar could bring massive inflation, depression and chaos. This may well be the Achilles Heel of modern capitalism. Another war may yet be fought over monetary matters, Cayce warned.

As for the new era, "With the changes that will be wrought, true Americanism, the universal thought that is expressed and manifested in the brotherhood of man, as in the Masonic Order, will be the eventual rule in the settlement of affairs of the world. Not that the world is to become a Masonic Order, but the principles that are embraced in same will be the basis upon which the new order of peace is to be established." (Case # 1152–11)

So the new order will be world-wide, and nations will peacefully "carry on their trade one with another". The exporting of modern technology—the Green Revolution in agriculture—can solve the problems of food in an expanding population. There is no shortage of land—indeed there is a surplus. Demographers' statistics reveal that the entire population of three and a half billion human beings in the world could be settled in an area the size of Alaska, with a half acre for each family of five. In the U.S., 70 per cent of the people live on just 2 per cent of the land. The solution is obviously one of decentralization of industries and a rural-urban balance.

Despite the scare tactics used in the "population explosion", it is hardly the threat some would have us believe. The problem is the *economic system of distribution* of the world's wealth of resources, of which there are more than enough. The great fear is that the need cannot be met under the present system. Alas, the public is not told this by a controlled press, one of censorship by ownership.

The exact kind of economic system in the coming new age is not spelled out in the Cayce readings, but the essentials of it are specific enough. It will be some type of "cooperative, coordinating" society, something on the order of our present consumers' and producers' co-ops. The evils of absentee, supercorporate ownership would thus be alleviated. The fad of communal living today is an indication; even the "Hippie" communes in the hills, if morally well-based, may point the way. But economically they will have their difficulties staying afloat in a sea of private monopoly capitalism. "Group capitalism" offers more hope, and we shall explore it at some length.

A quiet revolution has been taking place in American economic life, and it is bringing a new dimension to the free-enterprise system. The phenomenal boom of cooperative organizations, after decades of slow, unspectacular growth, is rejuvenating the old and cherished pioneer spirit of self-help and interdependence. And they may well be the answer to many of our social and economic ills. Moreover, they keep out the heavy hand of government.

Cooperative enterprises might just as aptly be called "People's capitalism". A sort of do-it-yourself mutual aid society, co-op members elect the board of directors which hires the management that employs members in a business which the customers own and operate for their own benefit. Their aim is to save money rather than make money in investments. Basically, cooperatives are run like any other business, although there are some important differences. They are motivated not by profit but by the idea of people acting together to help themselves. This sense of shared purpose is the soul of the organization. Running their own business affords members—most of whom could never go into business on their own—some democratic control over the operation and the end product. Whatever the number of shares one may own, the practice is "one member, one vote", which prevents the domination of the company by a few large shareholders.

Even in profit-making co-ops there is usually a limited return on capital invested by members. Profits are secondary, but there should be some for a reserve or future expansion. Benefits take many forms. In manufacturing, the chief asset may be jobs. In housing, memorial, and health associations, the main benefit is lower costs. In retail stores and farm co-ops, it is the cash return. But in all it is democratic control of the organization. The cash return is based on the amount of participation by the member, not on the number of shares he holds. A food store member who spent $1,000 a year there might receive these benefits: a 5 per cent year-end rebate, or $50; quality groceries at fair prices; a voice in the business; perhaps a job there.

Membership is open to all who want the services, regardless of race, creed, or colour. There are black, white, brown and mixed co-ops—and not all are in low-income brackets. Some apartment projects in élite neighbourhoods are very expensive indeed. The appeal is a broad one, and especially to the young and the frustrated.

Sprouting across the land are increasing numbers of community child-care centres, buying clubs, health clinics, credit unions, memorial societies, housing projects, retail stores, farms, processing plants. And they are rendering a distinctive service to their communities as well as their members.

The simplest kind of non-profit enterprise is the credit union, a cooperative lending institution chartered by the state or federal government. It may be formed by as few as 100 neighbours, plant employees, members of a church, labour union, fraternal order. They pool their savings, which will typically draw 5 per cent interest, and loan out to those members who need to borrow at 6.5 per cent. Members elect a board of directors, who serve without pay, a supervisory committee that audits the books, and a loan committee that passes on borrowers' requests. The treasurer, who manages the business, sometimes with the help of volunteers, may be the only paid employee.

One of the largest, Cooperative Centre Federal Credit Union, Berkeley, Calif., has accumulated $15 million in assets, affording its 21,000 members and 40 employees a deserved feeling of unity and accomplishment. A consumers co-op in a Negro neighbourhood of Chicago saved its members in a five-year period exactly $119,642.87 on the cost of furniture, which was shipped direct from factory to member. An apartment project with units that could easily rent for $300 month, pegged its price at $110; and members soon found it feasible to reduce their rent to $85. One bereaved family in a memorial society gratefully reported, after a member of the family died, that "The beautiful but simple casket . . . cost slightly under $100. Transportation, embalming, and other necessary expenses together with use of the chapel and organist came to just over $100." A sum far less than the $1,000 average cost of a funeral today.

A large housing project at Columbia Point, in Boston, has grown into an almost self-sustaining, self-governing community. It contains 1,500 units, with over 4,000 children and two schools in the neighbourhood. Members operate a library, credit union, meat buying club, a retail store. The co-op uses the Scandinavian "delegate" system, whereby the small voluntary groups combine to elect the governing board. Each operating unit sends one representative to meet with the board once a month, which is responsible for making policy. The board and officers are guided by and must persuade the many representatives in the "House of Delegates".

In Sweden, co-ops handle 15 per cent of the total production. Norwegian cooperatives do 11 per cent of the nation's retail trade. In Denmark, 90 per cent of all poultry and dairy products are sold through and to affiliated, coordinated co-ops, and small farmers have co-op machinery pools. For decades these countries have had stable economies, little inflation, no unemployment problems. And private enterprise still flourishes.

The oldest surviving cooperative was founded in Scotland in 1812. Since then, European co-ops have expanded from small retail stores to wholesale distribution to processing and manufacturing; from farms to slaughter houses to deep freezes. There are strong affiliated consumers' and producers' movements in West Germany, France, Italy, England, Ireland, Greece, India, Pakistan, Ceylon, Canada and most other nations of the "free" world. In the U.S. they have been around since 1845, but the current phenomenon has taken place since 1961, and especially in the past five years.

One of the newer co-ops is a modern supermarket in New York City. Opened in 1968, the Harlem River Consumers Cooperative offers quality groceries at fair prices and employs 45 dedicated people. Its founder, Negro attorney Cora Walker, was strongly motivated; she provided the necessary inspiration. "A big problem we have always had to endure was that the groceries were poor in quality and high in price," she recalls. "The situation was very discouraging. But the '64 riots taught me the need for something real. People must give of themselves. So help me, it's like a new religion. Self-help is absolutely essential. We must look at the problem, replace despair with hope, and get to work."

Disappointments and rebuffs were abundant in the beginning, mainly from inertia. "We had to go to the community first," she explained. "We had to find the ones who were dedicated. Fortunately, that turned out to be no problem. The one thing I under-estimated was the number of people in the neighbourhood who would be interested."

Mrs. Walker enlisted the help of enthusiastic teen-age boys and girls who within six weeks sold $10,000 worth of co-op memberships at $5 a share. By the time the store opened a year later, over $210,000 in memberships and $50 five-year debenture bonds had been sold to 3,200 persons, opening the way to $240,000 in cash or credit from outside sources. "I have found that big business is eager to participate when they are reassured that things are going to move," she said.

Big business has never had any love for co-ops, but confidence and support did come from Litton Industries, makers of grocery fixtures and equipment, and from Supermarkets General Corporation, operators of 79 Shoprite stores, who served as consultants from the beginning. Mid-Eastern Cooperatives and the Nationwide Foundation also played important parts.

But Cora Walker adds, "It was just the little people, mostly the poor ones, you understand, who had faith and parted with their hard-earned money. All their $5 investments made the store possible. More important, it made them part of it. This is Harlem's gift to Harlem. It's not a poverty programme. It's a people's programme—and they work hard . . ."

The store is open to the public, but members enjoy discounts on specials and receive dividends and rebates of about 5 per cent on their purchases. Annual sales volume is expected to exceed $2 million, and they are already contemplating more stores and perhaps as many as five in the future.

Cooperatives' chief needs are capital and technical assistance. They can succeed where there are adequate funds, credit or loan guarantees, and advice in management, accounting, marketing.

A new Federation of Southern Cooperatives has been formed to provide just this kind of help in the South. Some financial assistance has come from the Office of Economic Opportunity and the Ford Foundation along with outside technical advice. It has enabled 30,000 black farmers to expand their production, diversify crops, market their produce—and gain self-respect with their new economic freedom in 100 co-ops.

One of the first of the new-breed co-ops was Southern Consumers in LaFayette, La. Founded in 1961 by Father Albert McKnight, a Negro priest, it now has 2,500 members in Southern Louisiana. Since then some 400 agricultural cooperatives with a membership of 12,000 families have been formed and are operating in Louisiana, Mississippi, Alabama and Georgia.

Perhaps the best known is SWAFCA—Southern Alabama Farmers Cooperative Association—organized by veterans of the Selma March in 1967. Designed to produce vegetables, which largely defy the mechanization that displaced so many cotton workers, the programme absorbs great numbers of manual tillers and pickers. It now markets members' cotton also.

But SWAFCA met almost immediate reprisals from the white power structure in Alabama. Plants refused to sell fertilizer, lime trucks would not deliver, processing plants discontinued buying pickling cucumbers and peas from members; their trucks were harassed for "traffic violations", and the organization was attacked by local news media.

Yet SWAFCA in its infancy sold $50,000 worth of vegetables and gained $100,000 in credits from lending institutions. Its membership shot up to 1,800, and the OEO came through with a $400,000 grant. In 1969, its sales reached several hundred thousand dollars, with a potential of a $3 million crop. Now it is studying the feasibility of a freezing plant to market nationally its okra, peas, greens, sweet potatoes.

The International Independence Institute has a programme for land acquisition for the resettlement of landless sharecroppers and tenant farmers. It is convinced these people prefer to stay on the farm in a familiar environment rather than migrate to crowded cities. Robert Swann, its field director, believes that "many people in the ghettos now would undoubtedly like to return to the land", if they could make a living there.

Another organization now at work in the South is New Communities, Inc. It has started operations with 5,700 organic acres of farm land. A Georgia co-op, it plans to have such services as a medical centre, library, nursery school, community centre, store, and cooperative marketing for its members. Projections for the future, mostly privately developed and operated, include light industry such as food processing, plastics manufacturing, prefab housing.

Among the most successful co-ops are housing projects, of which there are now 700 serving some 250,000 families. Huge new developments for both lower and middle-income groups have gone up in New York City, Brooklyn, Jamaica, Detroit, Chicago, Washington. New York's "Co-op City" —Rochdale Village—a vast high-rise apartment development, can accommodate 15,300 families, largest of its kind in the world and the State's tenth biggest "city". Significantly, juvenile delinquency and school drop-out figures in such communities are far below those of the average metropolis.

Residents, some of whom are on welfare, take a new pride and initiative in "their" homes and "their" organization. A former mayor of Hometown, Ill., a Chicago suburb, congratulated his successor on the appearance of a newly acquired housing project purchased by the tenants. "They used to look so run-down before the co-op took over. Now they're a real asset," he said. For many members, the co-op is the only way they could hope to eventually own their home. Another experienced business executive looks upon cooperative housing as an inspiring programme to weave a "new fabric for community development" in America.

Retail co-ops are also on the upswing. Mostly food stores, there are 900 of them from Massachusetts to California. Now they are expanding into other merchandise lines such as furniture, hardware, clothing, drug and variety stores, laundromats. New York City has not only food stores but furniture, pharmacy and optical outlets. In Washington, D.C., there are 41 retail stores doing a $40 million annual volume. In 1957, there were 14 stores with $11 million gross sales. Cooperative Enterprises of Akron, Ohio, now operates six supermarkets and five optical centres. They dispense some 45,000 pairs of eyeglasses yearly.

Another phenomenon is the success of cooperative health associations, of which there are some 200. Group Health Cooperative of Puget Sound, Seattle, already over 100,000 strong, reports membership increasing at a rate of

1,000 a month. It opened three new medical clinics in one twelve-month period, 1967–8. Another, Health Insurance Plan of Greater New York, has 750,000 members. One of its outstanding participants, the Bedford-Williamsburg Medical Group, had a 50 per cent membership growth in one year, bringing its rolls up to 20,000 persons.

These medical plans usually provide for prepayment of premium, comprehensive care, consumer control and ownership with hired staff of physicians and nurses, and specialized group practice under one roof. The chief impetus, of course, is the atrocious high cost of medical care.

Rural electric co-ops, of which there are almost 1,000, are urging the decentralization of U.S. industry to attract it to smaller towns and achieve a rural urban-balance, alleviating some major problems in overcrowded cities. In 1968, the Chicago-based Cooperatives League of the USA initiated what could become a widespread rural co-op housing programme.

Contrary to the current astounding boom of cooperatives, the older farmers' co-ops of the Midwest are on the decline, as the small, family farmer disappears from the American scene in deference to giant corporate growers— the modern agri-business. The small business man may go the same way. But the one bright hope for the little farmer is in raising organic vegetables, now booming.

As Cayce predicted, cooperatives are already playing a new role in renovating our economic life. And they are showing the way to a new people's capitalism by bringing the alienated into the mainstream of the free-enterprise system. Polls reveal that 33 million Americans feel left out, and these disenchanted people attribute their frustration to lack of opportunity and the neglect of their plight by those in power. A way must be found to rally, encourage, inspire, make them feel that they "belong" and have a stake in the prosperity of the nation. America needs an ideology, a unifying of purpose. Economic cooperation might well be the catalyst, and prove to the world that American free enterprise—as distinct from subsidized monopoly enterprise —is truly free and enterprising. The ownership and management of business is everybody's business. Co-operators regard the movement as a major, middle-way bulwark

against state socialism and private cartels. In co-ops, everybody has a vested interest to defend, not just in terms of
money but in benefits.

The power structure has a history of opposing co-ops,
just as it has a history of dominating government—federal,
state and local. The late Murray Lincoln, former head of
Nationwide Insurance Company and a past president of the
Cooperative League, once felt compelled to say: "Cooperatives do not seek to change the form of political government
under which we live, since they themselves depend upon a
democratic society for their own existence. Authoritarian
societies insist upon control of their economic machinery
and do not allow people to set up associations to handle
their own economic affairs. Genuine cooperatives are possible only in a democratic society. They constitute a form
of economic democracy which supports political democracy."

The best way to guarantee both is to encourage participation of the people in a piece of the action.

Excessive private property and the accumulation of unneeded and unusable personal wealth—the source of most
of today's problems—would eventually lose their hold on
the American economy. Co-ops hold prices down and keep
them honest, ideas abhorrent to the price-fixers. The fact
that just 1.6 per cent of the populace owns 80 per cent of
all corporate stock is not healthy in today's climate. A
levelling must surely come. The many will not forever com-
placently stay in economic bondage to the few.

The hysterical Far-Right, the ultra-conservatives among
the big money interests, do not wish to face these realities,
and they succeed in convincing many unthinking small
business people to follow their propaganda line. They
righteously complain of Big Government, Big Spending,
Big Labour Unions. They never complain of big business,
big subsidies, big military contracts. The little man is unaware that their interests are not the same as his interests,
that his prosperity is dependent upon the prosperity of the
people about him, that the liberal view in the long run is
to his benefit. In short, he has been "taken". Unknowingly
to him, the conservatives believe in the "welfare state" of
government handouts of the people's money to big business; it is the social Welfare State for the common man that

they oppose. That comes under the category of "wasteful spending", and federal regulation of monopolies is "Government interference". Big money has a way of tarnishing whatever it touches. What we have is socialism for the rich and free enterprise for the poor.

But we live in a world of change—more rapid now than at any time in modern history. The very fact of our existence at this critical period in this particular place is not without meaning. We are all part of the Grand Design. If man is to have a better world in which to live, he himself will have to fashion it. He is his own greatest enemy. With his free will, he can choose to live by the law of the jungle, the survival of the fittest; he can even choose to defy God. Yet, said Cayce, "There are those conditions that in the activity of individuals, in line of thought and endeavour, oft keep many a city and many a land intact, through their application of the spiritual laws in their associations with (others).

"Tendencies in the hearts and souls of men are such that these upheavals may be brought about . . . It is true that man brings order out of chaos by his compliance with Divine Law. Or by his disregard of it, man brings chaos and destructive forces into his experience." (Case # 3976 series)

Indeed, we tend to be apathetic toward those things that do not concern or involve us in some personal way—a spiritual problem in itself, as are most problems in the final analysis. Our indifference is a measure of our own self-centredness. Mass complacency in public affairs, for instance, leaves a power vacuum quickly usurped by the few with special interests. So people generally get about the kind of government they deserve. But this day is passing; the future lies with the young, and they have shown that they are ready, willing and able to get involved. They are a generation of reformers and crusaders; but they need to temper their radicalism with prudence and an alternative. Extremists all, the Beatniks and the Peace-niks with their long hair, thongs, beads, medallions, even look like Atlanteans. Moreover, they have a strong innate interest in the Atlantis theory.

The nation may yet be able to right itself. Said Cayce:

"As the Spirit of God once moved to bring peace and harmony out of chaos (in the creation), so must the Spirit move over the earth and magnify Itself in the hearts, minds and souls of men to bring peace, harmony, and understanding, that they may dwell together in a way that will bring that peace, that harmony that can only come with all having the one Ideal . . .

"This is the whole law (love), this is the whole answer to the world, to each and every soul. That is the answer to the world conditions as they exist today." (Case # 3976 series)

But such togetherness is almost impossible in our divisive, competitive, mobile society. Millions of nomadic Americans have become rootless in the constant search of employment, moving from city to city every few months or few years. This fact of American economic life undermines stability, concern for community or neighbour, interest in civic or political affairs. It breeds an I-could-care-less attitude.

Whatever the New Order may bring, it must above all be just, and it must be stable, providing a feeling of unity, security, participation and belonging, rewarding not the most cunning and combative but the most able and productive.

It is debasing to the human spirit that the energies and talents of men should be so devoted to the random, preying search for economic security; and worse, to the vulgar pursuit of wealth and position for his own self-aggrandizement.

"Know that right, justice, mercy, patience . . . is the basis upon which the new world order MUST eventually be established before there is peace. Then, innately, mentally and manifestly in self prepare self for cooperative measures in all phases of human relations." (Case # 416–17)

CHAPTER TWELVE

REINCARNATION: THE CONTINUITY OF LIFE

So the saga of the aggressive and progressive Atlanteans, today, yesterday and tomorrow, comes to an end. Only time can prove or disprove the premises of our chronicle. Atlantis and reincarnation may not be the only answers to the perplexing problems of human existence in the earth, but they appear to be the best ones. Man not only expects life to be just; he expects it to make sense. The theories of Atlantis and human rebirth have the merit of resolving more questions than any other hypotheses yet put forth.

But two remain unexplored.

The heart of the problem concerning the meaning and purpose of life, the key to the dilemma of "Why are we here?" lies essentially in the existence or non-existence of the human soul. If man has no divine spirit, then we are, *ipso facto,* no more than advanced animals, an evolved race of intelligent primates. Life would be without real meaning or lasting purpose; a flick of existence in eternity and then no more. We would, in a word, be civilized animals, and that is all. Life would be much ado about nothing.

But the word *civilized* demands clarification. It portends vastly more than modern cities, communications, transportation, and gadgets. If it means anything it must mean the voluntary embracing of a moral code and the upholding of human rights and dignity. Man has will and reason, and he has conscience. He has ideals and principles and nobility. The three great precepts of life, Plato wrote, are Truth, Beauty and Goodness.

Why? Why for men? Which of the animals can appreciate truth, beauty or goodness? Beauty is relative, and it lies not so much in the thing seen as in the minds of those who see it. Goodness, and there is still a great deal of it in the world, is an impossible virtue outside the realm of divinity. And truth, that elusive abstraction, we can be sure has no attraction outside the human family. No chimpanzee has yet passed the first grade.

If we are simply educated animals we should have all

the animal instincts and little else. Life would be ruled entirely by the law of the jungle; muscular strength and shrewdness would be the only things that mattered. There would be no room and no reason for law and justice and decency; no pride, no ambition, no inventions, no trust; no music or creative art, no worship of the unseen. And man, wherever he has been found, has always felt the compelling need to pay homage to a higher being. If he was supreme in the earth, he must have inherited it; all he had to do was to look up to recognize his dependence, his inferiority.

Only a spark of the divine within the human breast can account for this civilization of man and the effort he expends in it. There is no satisfactory alternative in reconciling the present state of mankind, whatever the shortcomings, but to embrace the existence of the soul—that spark of spirituality that explains the extraordinary progress of man morally and culturally over the ages. It is, indeed, the motivating force that propels him onward and sometimes upward, making him a great deal higher than the animals and only a little below the angels. Man is the only animal that blushes, Mark Twain said, and the only one that needs to.

If man has a soul, a spirit, then he must be of spiritual origin, and there must be an origin—a universal force, being or consciousness. There must be a God, for the created demands a creator. The law requires a law maker. And there must be a meaning, a purpose in life other than just enjoying the fruits of the flesh. The "laws of nature" cannot be by accident.

If these things be true, then we are indeed strangers in the earth. And it is safe to assume that we would not be here without some sign, path, pattern or light to show us the way back home. Surely no father would ruthlessly abandon his children to the hazards of a cruel world of chance and ultimate oblivion. Surely there is a way out of the predicament in which man finds himself. Reincarnation and karma offer the most realistic solutions to this dilemma.

While the theory of rebirth is still to date unprovable scientifically, there are nevertheless numerous evidences of its validity. Some of these are of a material, tangible nature.

Almost everyone has at one time or another met new people or visited new places with the eerie feeling of reliving a past experience. Something deep within the unconscious memory seems to strike a familiar chord. The poet Shelley, while walking in a part of the country he had never visited before, remarked to a companion of his strange feeling of having been there before. "Over that hill", he said, "is an old windmill." They continued their stroll with expectation. Upon reaching the summit of the hill, the windmill came into view, and Shelley, a sensitive soul, fainted with emotion.

Dr. Hereward Carrington, the noted psychic investigator and author, reports the story of a man who visited an ancient castle for the first time. "There used to be a door here," the stranger said, pointing to a brick wall. No one knew of any such door, but later investigation revealed that centuries earlier there had indeed been a door there and that it had been bricked up.

All her life, Laure Reynaud of France made repeated references to a former life in a manor in a warmer climate —rich but tubercular. She vividly recalled the house and landscape. At the age of 45, she made her first trip to northern Italy, and in Genoa told a friend of her premonitions. "I know the very house!" he exclaimed. Upon arrival there, she said, "This is not the house, but it's not far away." With her guidance, they located the place she'd described. "Here is where I lived and died! However, I'm sure I was not buried in the cemetery, but interred in the Church." Family and burial records disclosed that the person she claimed to have been died an invalid in the house at Albaro and was buried in the Church of Notre Dame du Mont.

In the famous Shanti Devi case of Muttra, India, she recognized her former husband and relatives as well as the house and neighbourhood.

Many Americans will recall the five-year-old Chinese girl who toured this country giving piano concerts. The child had no musical training or even parental background in the art. She played by ear; yet her musical talent was incredible. She could play any composition after hearing it once, even though she had to stand up to the piano to reach the keyboard.

The most realistic answer to the phenomena of the genius is that the soul entity was accomplished in the art in one or more former lives. A similar answer explains the popular interest expressed in Civil War history; those who took part in it have now had time to reincarnate in considerable numbers. Thus the basis of the intuitive instincts of man is revealed.

The case of Ted Sterrett, a leather goods merchant in London, is an intriguing one. He loved to paint, but showed only mediocre talent. One night he visited a hypnotist to see if he could cure his asthma, but while in trance expressed his burning desire to paint well. The hypnotist, alert to the implications, promptly brought up an easel and suggested he paint. After an hour, Sterrett woke up, and to his surprise gazed upon a picture of an unfamiliar street scene in modern, abstract style. It was unlike anything he'd ever done before.

Sterrett placed the canvas in his shop, and a few days later a customer bought it, saying it was of a street in Milan, Italy, a city Sterrett had never visited. Encouraged, Sterrett returned to the hypnotist and, again under the influence, painted a strange picture showing a field of sawn-off tree stumps. He didn't know the meaning of it, but one day a foreigner came into the shop and said it was the burial ground of a South American Indian tribe. Sterrett continued painting. In one week he sold nineteen pictures, and a fashionable art gallery offered to hold an exhibition of his works.

The cases of Bridey Murphy, Irene Specht, and Jean Donnelson are well known. All under the influence of hypnosis discussed in intimate detail past lives in nineteenth century Ireland, ancient Egypt, and the American Civil War. Some of the explanations to refute their stories are more fantastic than the theory of reincarnation. Claims that the hypnotized subject will say almost anything to please the hypnotist are invalid. All three of them did not hesitate to answer in the negative to certain questions put in the affirmative, and some incorrect statements made by the operator were quickly corrected in no uncertain words.

Nor does the notion that they were getting their information from the minds of the hypnotists stand up. The hypnotists were simply not that well informed; they had little or no knowledge of the periods of history under discussion.

Most obvious of all, the human personality is far too deep, complex, contrary and eccentric to have been quickly attained. We are all peculiar people; some are just more peculiar than others. Many could not possibly get that way in just one lifetime! Heredity and genes may play a part, but they only tell How, not Why, for the physical, not the psyche.

Dr. Ian Stevenson, psychiatrist, of the University of Virginia, has investigated hundreds of cases of memories of past lives, and found at least 44 of them to be valid. But he is almost alone in American scientific circles. Paradoxically, a group in Czechoslovakia is similarly researching reincarnation. And the Soviet Union is now spending $13,000,000 a year on para-psychological research. The U.S. Government spends zero.

While we are still trying to "prove" ESP and the work of Dr. Rhine at Duke University, the Russians are exploring how it may best be used in communications, etc. They are attempting to control factors influencing *psi* (psychic ability), and their articles are published in scientific journals. Scientists give lectures on Cayce, Croiset, Serios and other psychics. (Cayce material was bootlegged into Moscow in 1960 by the author.) Their work in telepathy and telekinesis and hypnotism surpasses our own, and they have even developed a camera to photograph the aura, a phenomenon unrecognized by American scientists. Ostrander and Schroeder, in their book, *Psychic Discoveries Behind the Iron Curtain,* report that equipment for detecting an electrofield about the human body is being used at the Laboratory for Biological Cybernetics at the University of Leningrad.

The religious significance of all this is obvious. Ironically, the communists may be the first to scientifically establish the existence of the human spirit, i.e., the soul. Atheism would die a sudden death; yet orthodox religions might find themselves in an uncomfortable position.

From the reincarnationist view, the position of the

church today appears to be a precarious one. What it has to offer in answer to and explanation of human problems is generally vague, visionary, and unsatisfying. Intellectuals have become sceptics and left the church because the priesthood has lost the keys. All the evils and inequities of this cruel, harsh world will somehow be rectified in the nebulous "hereafter". Through some magic never quite explained, the "saved" will inherit eternal life—whether deserving of it or not. Such a "heaven" would, of course, have long ago become contaminated with the sins of the world, and therefore be no heaven at all. The "damned" will be condemned to limbo forever, although the Bible clearly states that "God has not willed that any soul should perish." Stranger still, the church puts much emphasis on immortality from birth *forward,* and fears immortality from birth *backward.*

But if the church were right in its orthodoxy, it is not assuming too much to say that the Creator is losing 99 per cent of his children—a most unlikely consequence. Eternity in "hell" is a long time for the repayment of misdeeds done in the few short years of this life. But the old fear-psychology of eternal "hell, fire and damnation" no longer suffices. For that reason it has largely been discarded in the modern pulpit for more liberal if ambiguous views.

It is true that the New Testament does not record that the historical Jesus (as distinct from the eternal Christ) taught directly the idea of reincarnation. But this does not necessarily mean that He didn't accept it or teach it; only that it is not so recorded in the present Bible. Indeed, immortality from the beginning seems to have been taken for granted. It was elementary knowledge among certain people, particularly the Essenes and the Gnostics. The striking thing is that the writers of the Bible never repudiated reincarnation or taught that it was false, although it was a current idea of the day and vigorously opposed by the Sadducees, the materialists.

Since the Cayce records affirm that Jesus was reared and tutored by Essenes, who accepted the continuity of life as a fundamental part of their doctrine, it is not too inconceivable that Jesus did not elaborate on this basic concept. Or, if He did teach it and it was duly recorded, it would certainly have been purged from existing manuscripts. A number of sources claim that this is what happened, although no responsible person makes the claim that all the Nazarene taught is in the Scriptures.

Dr. Leslie D. Weatherhead, the highly respected theologian of City Temple, London, has stated that "the early Christian Church accepted it (reincarnation) until the Council of Constantinople in A.D. 553, and then discarded it by a vote of 3 to 2. Even Origin, St. Augustine and St. Francis of Assissi accepted it." Origin (A.D. 185–254), one of the leading, early Christian scholars, was among those excommunicated for his views on the immortality of the soul. They were victims of the many Anathemas of the day.

The supposition that each birth into the earth plane is a new, special creation is man-made. The single-life idea is, therefore, a direct result of the diluted version of Christianity. There is little to support the notion in nature, in the Bible, or in human life itself. Nature constantly displays the continuity of life, e.g., trees "die" in the fall and come "alive" in the spring; the cycle of rainfall repeats itself; new days are "born."

When Christianity was popularized by the church fathers in the early centuries, several sources claim the doctrine of reincarnation was dropped. Only the Cabala, the secret religion of the Jews and the bible of the Gnostics, retained it, for the Essenes by then were extinct. Since few were aware of it, it would die out with the priesthood. Its knowledge was not considered desirable for the common people. Too, the burden of responsibility was shifted from the individual to Jesus to allow for an easy religion, attractive to the masses. Christianity was formalized and dogmatized —toned down to fit man as a religious system because man was not up to fitting it spiritually.

Their reasoning was sound if not ethical. Materialistic as man was, he would tend to say, "Why worry about this life—there are other lives to live," overlooking the consequences of karma—the law of cause and effect, of retributive justice. He would use it as an excuse for his shortcomings. Moreover, reincarnation would weaken the priesthood's ecclesiastical position of power and authority, and there would not be the same force behind the doctrine of submission. It was therefore deleted, and perhaps wisely for that day and age.

Still in the Vatican as well as in the pyramids is the full story of the eternal evolution of the soul, says Cayce, although it will not be completely revealed until man is spiritually mature and ready to receive it with the understanding and responsibility that is attached to it. The few have always known the whole truth from the very beginning.

But those who recognize the validity of the continuity of life should not make the mistake of maliciously condemning the church. For it has carried the torch for two thousand years. It has preached the message of love and taught the brotherhood of man and the Fatherhood of God, although not always perfectly. The fact that it does not now embrace a more profound philosophy is as understandable as it is regrettable. We should therefore be fair in our appraisal of the church's position. The clergy and the theologians of our day are not personally responsible for what happened in the sixth century, although the hierarchies long ago joined the money-changers on the temple steps. "The church is not perfect," as Billy Graham put it, "and if it were it would be imperfect the minute you joined it." Yet he preaches the vaguest of doctrines.

So the church, having lost influence and stature over the years, is in a quandary of its own making. Now it must pay the price for its past deficiencies and excesses. Karma! "Standing on the Promises of God" meant no more than Sitting on the Promises.

Indeed, it may find itself in an untenable and embarrassing posture when the truth of reincarnation is established beyond a reasonable doubt. The Dead Sea Scrolls or some other ancient manuscript yet to be uncovered may be the means of this. What the church will then do is a matter of conjecture. In the meantime, the best position it can take is one of openmindedness on the subject, thereby leaving the way open for a more graceful change in doctrine.

The Bible is replete with the theme of eternal life, the immortality of the soul, the creation of man in the beginning. The word *resurrection* in its original sense, says Cayce, meant reincarnation, and many New Testament texts carry a more profound meaning if considered in this context. The idea is not new, but it opens up for the Bible student a new horizon of understanding, casting light on shadowy passages never otherwise adequately explained. Indeed, without reincarnation many others go begging for plausibility. Our use of the word, however, should not be confused with transmigration, the belief of some Hindus that the soul may also return in the animal kingdom.

But reincarnation in itself is not important; does not contradict the Bible; does not change the basic ideals of Christianity or Judaism. What is important is its by-product —Karma.

Long have people wondered, Why the inequality of men? Why are some born into an environment offering every blessing—money, education, opportunity, the advantages of a happy home—while others enter the world in poverty, ignorance, sorrow, deformed bodies? Why should one be rewarded with intelligence or talent, another penalized with a dull mind or ill health at the very start of life, through no cause of their own and for conditions beyond their control? Where is the justice of a just God?

Each individual is born with a personality all his own— a mixture of good and bad traits which manifest at an extremely early age. They are carry-overs from previous experiences. But if there is no pre-existence of the soul, then these characteristics are not brought in by the entity and are not truly his own; they were forced upon him first by heredity and later by environment. Can he justly be held responsible by the Creator for urges and weaknesses which are not really his own, which came about by circumstances beyond his control?

Karma holds the unique distinction of affording the only answer to such questions. "He that leadeth into captivity shall go into captivity, he that killeth with the sword must be killed with the sword," is meaningless from the view of the one life. "Life for life, eye for an eye, tooth for tooth." These old rules of ancient law would be myths. But with the law of karma they are truths that become literal with reincarnation.

Karma is cause and effect in action, as exemplified in "As ye do unto others so shall it be done unto thee." There is no evasion of karma. "Be not deceived; God is not mocked: for whatsoever a man soweth, that shall he also reap." As the Nazarene said: "For verily I say unto you, till heaven and earth pass, one jot or one tittle shall in no wise pass from the law, till all be fulfilled." And, "I tell thee, thou shalt not depart thence, till thou hast paid the very last mite." And again, "Verily I say unto you, this generation shall not pass away till all be fulfilled." Man must pay to the last farthing for his transgressions, and the generations of man in the earth shall not cease until all has been met, until all has been fulfilled. He can learn only by doing, for he truly knows only what he has experienced. Growth comes through adversity.

With the continuity of life, God is truly a God of mercy, of justice, and most of all, patience. "Be ye therefore perfect", a seemingly impossible admonishment, is one of the most frequently recurring tenets in the Scriptures.

Thus people's lives follow a self-made pattern, a karmic pattern of loves, hates, fears, desires; of families, friends, groups and nations. Every soul has its own particular karmic pattern, says Cayce. These are of two types and are brought in at birth, which like death is but the transition to another plane of existence. There are those innate mental urges derived from experiences out-of-the-body in the cosmic realms, and the emotional tendencies builded from lives in the earth. The word *interests* most adequately describes the mental inclinations gained from planetary sojourns, while *feeling* best expresses those emotional urges from past physical lives—a kind of sensing or knowing without reason.

This is why men are such complex beings. Each thought, each word, each act adds to the total structure of his nature and becomes a part of his karmic pattern, Cayce insisted. Mind is the builder, and no effort is ever wasted. Thought upon thought, line upon line, we build that which we are and will be in the future. The circumstance in which we find ourselves is exactly that which we have earned; it is what we need or deserve. And what we do today will be meted out to us in like measure in some future life, for man is indeed the captain of his soul, the creator of his fate. In the words of that wise old axiom, "The mills of the gods grind slowly, but they grind exceedingly fine."

There is "good and bad" karma. Happiness, friends,

health, talents and prosperity are "good" karma. Disease, sorrow, handicaps, poverty are "bad" karma. Man instinctively considers good fortune his inherent right; he takes his positive karmic conditions as a matter of course, suggests Dr. Gina Cerminara in the best volume on the subject (*Many Mansions*). But the negative karma—illness, tragedy, misfortune, he immediately questions. Why did my child die? he asks, not realizing there is also karma for parents.

Every effect has its cause. Little happens by chance. Accidents are the rare exception, not the rule. When man realizes he is paying for even his most secreted thoughts and deeds, and will pay for them in the future, he will learn not only the wisdom but the necessity of right living. Karma is the operation of a law so ordered and precise as to guarantee justice always. Its purpose is moral education, to produce spiritual growth and strength, and it is created every day for better or for worse. We are constantly spinning new karma for ourselves in the choices we make, the decisions we reach. Sometimes the reaction is almost immediate; more often it is delayed in this life or the next. An indulgent life, for instance, usually requires years before premature dissipation sets in. A nation that brings war on another, will have war brought upon it, said Cayce.

"Bad" karma is the meeting of debts, the overcoming of deficiencies, the tempering of extremes. It is generated by intemperance, neglect, pride, greed, jealousy, and hate in all its forms. Unless it is met and the motivations behind it overcome, it can be a vicious cycle turning up again and again in the lives of its creator.

Forgiveness is one of the cardinal themes of the Bible. Often it is the only way to stop negative karma. "Forgive, and ye shall be forgiven," writes Luke. Why? To retaliate is to throw fresh fuel on the fire, generating new karma for the doer of the latter deed. It perpetuates evil. "Vengeance is mine," said the Lord. "For with the same measure that ye mete withal it shall be measured to you again," warns Luke.

While the law of karma is specific in operation, it does not always run in chronological order. It may be delayed several lifetimes—until the right set of circumstances occurs at a time when the entity is spiritually prepared to meet it.

Souls and groups of souls return by law or by will, but not with automatic regularity. Karmic problems with other persons may be delayed to conform with their incarnations. Any close association of long standing is almost certain to be karmic, good or bad.

In the long run, there is no "bad" karma, only good, since its purpose is spiritual growth. As in going to the dentist, it may hurt for a while, but you'll be so much better for it. Good karma is the result of patience, understanding, kindliness, cheerfulness, devotion, hard work, generosity, concern—the fruits of the spirit. If one is looking for perfection, he should start with himself!

The world has in it many people who are without hope, who are undernourished and poorly housed, who are frustrated and disenchanted. Whatever the causes, material and spiritual, we must not turn away from their needs, for we are indeed our brother's keeper, says Cayce. In sharing another's burden, in trying to right wrongs, one renders not only a service to others but creates good karma for himself and perhaps a better society. That is why it is better to give than to receive.

Sex, race, colour and religion may change from one incarnation to another, although the same sex is usually maintained. Consequently, the futility and the foolishness of intolerance is apparent. We only condemn ourselves when we express prejudices against others. Thus, reincarnation and karma destroy once and for all whatever grounds there may be for racial or religious intolerance. All men are brothers, there is no other real relationship.

Like rungs of a ladder, there are many degrees of developing souls—souls who have not assimilated the balancing factors of the earthly and planetary experiences; souls who are not aware that the will may use or misuse each opportunity presented. Anywhere along the evolutionary path men may slip and fall backward, carrying others with them. This is what happened in Atlantis, and it brought corruption, moral decay, eventual destruction to an empire infatuated with its power and authority. Its arrogance was inexhaustible.

Some Atlanteans became forces for evil in their abuse of others through the electrical and psychic powers available to them. In eras when electricity, hypnosis, psychology were not available, this corruption of character could not be completely redeemed, suggests Dr. Cerminara, a psychologist. Hence, those who misused this power cannot be said to have transmuted their greed and lust for supremacy unless, when offered the same opportunity under approximate conditions, they can use them constructively. "The cyclic progress of mankind has made the twentieth century just such a period. . . . Atlanteans are incarnating at present in great numbers. The amazing technology of the present age can therefore be understood . . . as the consequence of the bold, inventive genius of egos who brought with them a remembrance of Atlantean achievements."

The present is the testing period, she writes, "to determine whether in the intervening centuries they have acquired qualities that will withstand the renewed temptation to selfishness and civilized barbarity". It is the first opportunity they have had to meet the karma of that particular period. In the meantime, they have had chance after chance to accumulate the necessary wisdom and combative qualities. What they do now will decide the fate of the nation and the world.

One can only shudder in horror and dismay when contemplating the hierarchies of the Pentagon, CIA, and Wall Street, who hold such awesome power in their hands. Their combative qualities are in evidence but of the wrong sort. Their vision and wisdom appear, however shrewd and clever they may be, to calibrate at something less than 20–20.

But karma is not a fatalistic attitude, although in India it has become such to the detriment of many of its people. The will is always supreme. It is the will that accepts or rejects the choices and opportunities presented, for that is its birthright in each experience. The will is the governing factor, and it may alter the pattern and the destiny builded by a soul's previous activities. Through karma, a predetermined set of conditions is certain, but by will and reason these are often subject to alteration. Thus both free will and predestination exist in a person. We are like the bear in the zoo; he can run back and forth, to and fro with complete freedom, but there are limits beyond which he cannot go.

If we fail in the exacting classroom of this life, we must return and go through the grade again, for to enter "heaven" without first gaining the necessary lessons would defeat our purpose. We would not only find ourselves in an environment with which we could not cope, but one in which we would be at an embarrassing disadvantage.

Reincarnation and karma give man a new hope and a new understanding in his struggle for the better life and a better world. The Bible, that most remarkable of all books, takes on a new meaning. The seeming inequality of men, physically and mentally, is vindicated, as is the "injustice" of a just God. The injustice rests with men. What appears to be "luck", "unfairness", "accident" is rooted in more solid ground than mere chance or the mischievous doings of a whimsical Creator.

Extracts from the Cayce Readings

"Here we have truly a pathological condition and a psychological one as well, and it extends to karmic reactions also (Asthma). For one doesn't press the life out of others without at times seeming to have same pressed out of self."

(Case # 3906–P–1)

"Here we find a physical expression of wantonness and selfishness in the past manifested in the present in the lack of physical, mental and spiritual faculties (mongoloid). The entity (in high position of authority) turned away from those who were without hope, who were disturbed in body and mind; the entity turned to the joys of the appetites in self. Here we find that the entity is overtaken, and what he has sown he is reaping.

". . . For through your (the parents) love and service, the soul-consciousness of this entity may become *aware* of what true abiding love leads individuals to do concerning those who are dependent upon others for every care; for the soul of this entity is entering an awakening in the present. Sow the seeds of truth, hope, of mercy, kindness and patience, making known by *application* the truth to this soul that 'I am my brother's keeper'."

(Case # 2319–P–1)

"The law of cause and effect is here being demonstrated (Multiple Sclerosis). Karmic conditions are being met. For as given of old, each soul shall give an account of every idle word spoken. It shall pay every whit. The entity is at war with *itself*. All hate, all malice, all that will make man afraid must be eliminated from the mind. . . .

"When the body becomes so self-satisfied, so self-centred as to renounce, refuse, not change its attitude; so long as there are hate, malice, injustice, those things which produce hate, which produce jealousies, which are at variance to patience, long-suffering, brotherly love, kindness, gentleness, there cannot be a healing of this body. What would it be healed for? That it might gratify its own physical desires and appetites? That it might add to its own selfishness?"

(Case # 3124–P–1)

"Don't let it occur again in this life (vehement, self-righteous intolerance), for there will be tendencies for drink—not only in yourself but in those about you. For that which ye hate has come upon thee. Don't hate *anything* in the present."   (Case # 8059–L–1)

"For each entity in the earth is what it is because of what it has been! And each moment is dependent upon another moment. So a sojourn in the earth, as indicated, is a lesson in the school of life."   (Case # 2823–L–2)

"Question: Is there anyone else with whom we could be as happy, or happier, in marriage, than with each other?

"Answer: Oh, we might name twenty-five or thirty such, if you choose to make it so! Marriage is what you make it! There is an experience to be worked out here, if you want to do it now. Since you have to do it sooner or later, you might as well do it now—if you want to. . . ."

(Case # 2525–L)

"We find that all conditions existent in physical bodies are produced by that which may be met. There are, in truth, no incurable conditions, though the mode of the plane's existence may be changed. That which exists is, and was, produced from a first cause; it may be met, counteracted, changed.

"For each ailment is the result of the breaking of a law. The healing will of necessity come when there is the compliance with other laws which meet the needs. The healing depends upon the individual and the attitude toward conditions from all angles; it depends upon the perception or the consciousness which may be manifested through the individual. . . .

"The evasion of a law puts off that condition which must eventually be met." (Case # 3744)

"For anger can destroy the brain as well as any disease. For it is itself a disease of the mind!"

(Case # 470–37, P–28)

"Before this we find the entity was in the land of the present nativity, and during those periods of turmoils and strife—in that called the Civil War. The entity was among the southern contingents, acting in the capacity of what is called the commissary, or one providing provisions for the handling of those who served in the capacity of soldiers.

"Thus we find the entity met many of those disturbing conditions, many of those in activities that brought the weighty problems of considering manners and means of distribution, as well as those influences from which resources might be obtained.

"The name then was Carl Brickner. In the experience the entity gained, for the sincerity of purpose was manifested in the manner in which the entity conducted himself."

(Case # 10, 225–CA)

CHAPTER THIRTEEN

THE HUMAN DESTINY

In man's study of himself and his relation to the whole, there comes an awakening to the full concept of the part he must play in the immense scheme of creation. While he may be baffled by what appears to be an extraordinary division of force in matter, there is always open to him a door through which he may pass to obtain the new vision. The door, of course, leads to his own inner self. He must come to understand this infinite, higher-dimensional self and his relation to his Source.

God, say the Cayce readings, is the one elemental life-essence, spirit, creative force—the *élan vital,* with its manifestation called mind. Mind includes not only man's physical form of mind—the three-dimensional, self-conscious viewpoint—but also the fourth, fifth and higher dimensional viewpoints of other planes of awareness. The mind of God embraces the one total life energy—what we call nature—with its universally evolved portion called mind in all its forms, all its stages of development, and all of its self-conscious, individual viewpoints—ourselves. In matter the highest manifestation is man; in spirit it is soul, and they are essentially one and the same. While in matter, man does not possess the Creator's kind of mind, but the kind that finds expression in its three divisions: the conscious; the subconscious or unconscious; and the superconscious. The latter is of the soul force, the spirit, and is often in conflict with the conscious mind of the temporal world. Yet in the end it must triumph.

All force, all power, all in the beginning and the end is of one Source. Matter, seemingly solid, when reduced to its smallest components is only energy of an electro-spiritual nature. The divisions which seem so evident in the physical are due to two causes: first, the rebellion of man against the Creative Will, both in and out of the material world—even though God's Will always has influence through and upon entities passing in the various planes—Mercury, Mars, Jupiter, Neptune, Venus, Saturn, Uranus, which are related to seven endocrine glands, the storehouses of karma. And second, the limitations of the conscious faculties in matter, or space-time, for man lives in a three-dimensional world. The five senses are not infallible; there are sounds he does not hear and colours he does not see.

The seeming complexity of existence in the earth plane not withstanding, the original impulse, the force which gave the soul its being in the beginning will manifest and dominate throughout any experience if given the opportunity of expression. The soul, left to itself, will carry out the will of its Creator. Spirit will conquer matter.

Like begets like, Cayce said. Being of God, man should strive to fully express that Presence, that Spirit which is within him. Thoughts are deeds. What one continually thinks he becomes; what one pursues in heart he makes a part of his being. Through the blood cells he builds in the physical by way of the glands that which the spirit and soul must feed upon and contend with. For the attributes of the soul and spirit are as many, and as many more, as the attributes of the mind, and they may be awakened by earnestly seeking after the fruits of the spirit.

It is not knowledge that builds the soul, but the understanding and the application of it to the opportunities presented in daily living. It is not what one knows, not what one professes to believe that matters so much, but what one *practises*. The soul will eventually meet itself upon whatever foundations it has builded. The point of expression may be in matter or in any of the other planes of disembodied consciousness, but the mind, ever the builder, is always the motivating force which acts through all planes. What man does in the physical is met in the physical, what is done in the mental is met in the mental, what is done in the spirit is met in the spirit.

Only the will of man can keep him from the realization of the Divine unity. Nothing separates him from his Maker but himself. From the very beginning it has been self, the ego, that has been the undoing, the downfall of man, and it is only through self that man, the "Prodigal son", may regain that status which was his in the beginning. The Christ soul came to show him the way—the means of attaining again his real, his spiritual, his natural home. Thus by his own free will and reason, man either adheres to or contradicts Divine law. And they are immutable laws, set between the Creator and the created.

All building, developing, growth, must come from within, engineered by mind, for each cell in the atomic force of the body is as a world of its own, and each cell being in perfect unison will build that necessary to reconstruct the physical and spiritual forces of the body. Spirit is in all matter, and it is electrical in function, regardless of the physical form it may take. It is subject to God's will, and through the mind, to man's will. Man is given, therefore, that necessary to be lord over all—and he is the only survivor of this creation. God has not willed that any soul should perish, but man in his headstrongness often hearkens to that which would separate him from his Maker, says Cayce.

With the gaining of the understanding of that within and its source, there comes the awakening, the development of the spiritual entity, and there must follow an attaining of the higher physical, mental and spiritual balance. When the body is no longer a hindrance to the free expression of the soul, when the conscious mind merges with the subconscious or unconscious, and the soul is as free in matter as out of it, the earth cycle is finished and the entity goes on to new adventures. The will conforms with the will of the Creator. Thus the evolution of force in vibration, of spirit in matter, is brought up to the point wherein man becomes one with the Creative Energy, or the Godhead.

His purpose then, stress the readings, is to evolve himself onward and upward until he again incorporates his mind and his spirit with the one complete Whole, while yet conscious of his own separate individuality. That is the whole meaning and purpose of life. That is man's destiny —to become one with his Maker, to again be worthy of and companionable to the Creator. It is not only possible and desirable that he attain the realization of the Oneness of All, it is necessary that he do so, however long it may take. In the growth through eternity's realm, a finite force of creation in the end becomes one with the Whole, for a cell, an atom or a vibration, like the raindrop, is never lost but must eventually become one with the Universal Forces. Nothing is ever lost or destroyed, only its form changed.

To reach this state of near-perfection requires at least thirty incarnations in the physical, plus all the stages of development gained in the other planes. And that gained in the cosmic realms must be proved in the material, for the earth is the testing place, the world of trial for the entire universal vibration. Without passing through each and every stage of evolution, there is not the raising of the vibration within to the point where it enables the entity to become one with the Whole. Man cannot reach perfection in matter; on the contrary, he often traps himself in it, unable to resist its temptations. Hence, in the growth throughout the system each stage is, must be manifest in the flesh.

The earth is the proving ground. Man must show his development in this plane until he has reached that stage of evolution wherein he may manifest through the higher spiritual planes en route to perfection, when Grace—the forgiveness of past sins—comes into effect. The law of karma is then abrogated.

The planets of the solar system have an influence, not because of their position at time of birth, but because of the soul's visitations there between incarnations. Many aspects of modern astrology are therefore overdrawn.

What one thinks, what he puts his mind to work upon, to live with, to feed upon, to abide with, that his soul-body becomes. It he dwells on moral, ethical, spiritual things he will become spiritual-minded, thereby narrowing the chasm between him and his destiny. There are no short cuts; there is no easy religious formula, no psychedelic drug experience, no mental gymnastics that will supplant this.

The change, the evolution, the growth takes place so that the entity may once again become one with the Maker. This is what the man Jesus, the elder brother, did in order to show the way. Taking on flesh many times, with all its desires and temptations, He became perfect in body, mind and soul as the Christ, and one with the Creator in spirit and in purpose, although not in identity.

For man to become one with the Father requires the same state of perfection in which he was created in the beginning, albeit much wiser. The theme is reiterated throughout the Bible. In Genesis, the Lord said to Abram,

"I am the Almighty God; walk before me, and be thou perfect." Deuteronomy states it as, "Thou shalt be perfect with the Lord thy God." In Ephesians it is, "Till we all come in the unity of the faith, and of the knowledge of the Son of God, unto a perfect man, unto the measure of the stature of the fullness of Christ." Matthew puts it pointedly. "Be ye therefore perfect, even as your Father which is in heaven is perfect." And in Romans, Paul sums it all up briefly: "The Spirit itself beareth witness with our spirit, that we are the children of God: And if children, then heirs; heirs of God, and joint heirs with Christ; if so be that with Him, we may also be glorified together."

That is the destiny of man; to regain that which he was and was intended to be—one in spirit and in purpose with the Whole, although not identical.

This does not mean he will lose his identity, for each will forever retain his own individuality, his own free will and reason, but it will be in accord with the will of God. While existing as a part of the Whole in an harmonious state of relative perfection with like souls, the entity will nevertheless be independent and separate, aware of its own individuality. But not without tasks!

All men are gods in the making, endowed with the wisdom and the power of creative thought, for souls are but atoms in the body of God. They may become co-exist-ent and co-creators with Him, becoming lords of, rulers over any of the various spheres through which souls pass. They may at any point in the earth or elsewhere, lead the way for their brother souls. Some highly developed souls return to the flesh, by choice, for this very purpose alone.

Thus there is a way out of the dilemma in which man finds himself. His destiny lies within, for *life is spirit in action,* and it is eternal.

By whatever route man may travel, he must in the end return to his Source, for the destiny of life is in Him who gave it. That is his goal, and along the way the path offers a higher, a more noble state of existence for all men. Man's laws will eventually coincide with God's laws. For always the struggle, the growth is upward toward the Light— little by little, line upon line, and in the process it makes the world a better place in which to live.

Although he may sometimes falter and slip backward,

man will surely move step by step out of the darkness into the light—led by that divine spark within.

Extracts from the Cayce Readings

"God is the beginning and the end of that which was brought into material manifestation, into that which is known as the plane from which man reasons in the finite. He is the Alpha and the Omega—the beginning and the end. God, the Father, the Spirit, the influencing force in every activity, is not wholly sufficient unto man's salvation, in that he, man, is a free-will being, as intimated—Alpha, beginning; Omega, ending—for the separation, the confirmation, the segregation, the building, the adding to, are necessary in relation to those activties that lie between the beginning and the end."   (Case # 8337)

"Man reaches that stage in the material plane of being aware of what he does with and about his consciousness of the knowledge, the intelligence of the First Cause; and he makes or produces that which is known as the entering into the first cause, principle or essence, that there may be demonstrated that which gains for the soul, that which would make the soul acceptable, companionable to the Creative Force.

"As each entity, each soul passes from one plane of consciousness to another it becomes aware of self and that sphere to which it attains. Hence, the entity develops through the varied planes of the earth and its solar system. A soul is as real as a physical body and is as subject to laws as the physical body. Personal experience has its influence upon the inner soul. In the material, mental and spiritual experiences of souls, it is found that there are those influences that have their effect upon the thought of those who would do this or that. Who gives it? Self! Just as when an entity fills its mind with those things that add to the carnal forces, so does the mind become the builder throughout, and the physical mind becomes carnally directed.

"Mind is the builder ever, whether in the spirit or in the flesh. If one's mind is filled with those things that bespeak of the spirit, that one becomes spiritual-minded. As we may find in a material world; envy, strife, selfishness, avarice are the children of man; long suffering, kindness, brotherly love, good deeds are the children of the spirit. Choose ye whom ye will serve.

"As an individual in any experience, in any period, uses that of which it is conscious in relation to the laws of the Creative Forces, so does that entity develop towards a companionship with the Creator.

"He that looks within is higher, for the spirit knoweth the Spirit of its Maker, and the children of same are as given. 'My Spirit beareth witness with thy spirit', saith He who giveth life. What is life? A manifestation of the First Cause—God!"   (Case # 720–CA)

"What is thy God? Are thy ambitions set only in whether ye shall eat tomorrow, or as to wherewithal ye shall be clothed? Ye of little faith, ye of little hope, that allow such to become the paramount issues in thine own consciousness! Know ye not that ye are His? For ye are of His making! He hath willed that ye shall not perish, but hath left it with thee as to whether or not ye become even aware of thy relationship with Him."   (Case # 281–41)

"The entity entering the earth plane, and manifesting in the flesh, is banished unto Saturn when such conditions are shown in the body that the spiritual entity merits that condition in the earth's solar system to which all insufficient matter is cast for the remoulding, as it were. . . .

"We find the relations given from those spheres as in Mercury, Venus, Mars, Jupiter, Earth, Uranus, and Neptune. There is the changing from one development to another until the entity passes from the solar system through Arcturus or Septimus. . . .

"In the earth's plane that entity who manifests such hate, such aggrandizement of the laws of the flesh that any desire is made unnatural, has a reclamation, a remoulding, a beginning again in the spheres of Saturn's relative forces."
(Case # 8337–47/11)

"When the Prince of Peace came into the earth for the completion of His own development in the earth, He overcame the flesh and temptation. Thus He became the first of those who overcame death in the body . . . to so illuminate and revivify the body that He could take it up again—even when the fluids of the body had been drained away . . ."   (Case # 1152–L–2)

"Why came He into the earth to die the death, even on the Cross? Has it been, then, the fulfillment of promise, the fulfillment of man's estate? Else why did He put on flesh and come into the earth in the form of man, but to be one with the Father; to show man his divinity, man's relationship to the Maker; to show man that indeed the Father meant it when He said, 'If ye call I will hear. Even though ye be far away, even though ye be covered with sin, if ye be washed in the blood of the lamb ye may come back.' Then, though He were the first of man, the first of the sons of God in spirit, in flesh, it became necessary that He fulfill *all* those associations, those connections that were to wipe away in the experience of man that which separates him from his Maker."   (Case # 3014–CA)

"(As the Master spoke) He that *abideth in me* hath indeed then put on Christ, hath indeed become one with Christ and is no longer subject to the temptations of the world, and hence becomes one with Him . . . To such there is no returning to the flesh."   (Case # 2094–CA)

"We find that there are no chance coincidents. Each and every individual follows out that line of development of the entity in the present earth plane which it has received from the preceding conditions. Each grain of thought or condition is a consequence of other conditions created by self."   (Case # 8337–46/51)

"Not in the amount of moneys, lands, holdings, houses, cattle or gold; but in the ability to serve thy brother lies strength, security, and the perfect knowledge of God."
                              (Case # 900–D301)

"How can ye do His bidding? Not in mighty deeds of valour, not in the exaltation of thy knowledge or power; but in the gentleness of the things of the spirit . . . Wilt thou separate thyself? For there is nothing in earth, in heaven, in hell, that may separate thee from the love of God, of thy brother, save thyself.

"Then, be up and doing, knowing that as thou hast met in life those things that would exalt thy personal self, these ye must lose in gentleness, in patience. For in patience ye become aware of your soul, your individuality lost in Him, your personality shining as that which is motivated by the consciousness of thy Lord and Master.

"Thus does your destiny lie within yourself, and the destiny of the world."   (Case # 281–56)

APPENDIX

The phenomenon of Edgar Cayce's life is only slightly less phenomenal than his readings. As a youth he had some mystifying experiences: talking to invisible playmates on a regular, recurring basis; sleeping on his spelling book and memorizing every word of it including the copyright date; telling his mother what to do for a hurt; conversing with an angelic "presence" that physically wasn't there.

The only son in a church-going, "Campbellite" family of five children, Edgar Cayce was born on a farm near Hopkinsville, Kentucky, in 1877. A poor student, he received no more than a grammar school education, and eventually took up photography as a trade. His psychic powers were accidentally discovered in 1901, when he was twenty-four. He caught a cold and suddenly lost his voice. After a year of numerous and unsuccessful medical treatments, he became resigned to a life of rasping whispers.

About this time hypnotism was enjoying a fad throughout the country, and a friend suggested that he try it as a means of helping his condition. Cayce was willing to try anything that might cure his throat. A local hypnotist offered his services, and Edgar readily accepted. He insisted, however, that he put himself to sleep, with the friend making the suggestions after he was "under".

The experiment proved to be more than successful. Cayce went into a deep trance and described the condition in his vocal cords, advising, strangely enough, what to do for it. The advice was followed by the hypnotist—that of suggesting the blood circulation increase to the affected area—and when Cayce awakened he had regained his normal speaking voice. After a number of follow-up sessions, the cure turned out to be a permanent one.

Cayce, his family and his friend were astounded. When word got around of this unusual occurrence, he was besieged with requests by the sick to try his diagnoses and curative methods on them. He was reluctant to attempt anything of the kind. In the first place, he was uneducated and knew nothing of medicine or anatomy in his waking state; moreover the hypnotist giving the suggestions was not a trained medical man. For all Edgar knew he might prescribe something that would kill somebody! After all, he had no idea what went on while he was asleep. In the end, however, he gave his consent, and his misgivings proved unfounded.

With authoritative certainty, he successfully described without prior information, a tilted stomach, an engorged spleen, ulcers in specific places in the stomach, pinworms, pregnancy, anaemia, diabetes, epilepsy, misplaced vertabra, and almost every other known, and unknown, ailment. The information was accurately couched in medical terminology, and the treatments suggested seemed to get results.

In most of the cases that developed over the years, the celebrated psychic never met the persons making the requests. They were received through the mail; the recipients of the readings were usually hundreds of miles away. All Cayce needed was the full name of the person, his address, and where he would be at the appointed time of the reading. Lying on the couch with his necktie and shoelaces loosened—for better circulation, the readings said—he could answer any question put to him. His wife, Gertrude, usually made the suggestions and asked the questions, while his lifelong secretary, Gladys Davis, took everything down in shorthand. After a while, the sleeping Cayce would start to mumble, as though searching for something. Then he would clear his throat and speak in a firm, authoritative voice. "Yes, we have the body", he would begin, and then go into a half-hour discussion of the physical condition of the person who was ill.

The Cayce files are replete with unfathomable cases. One of the earliest, in 1906, was for a college football player who walked off the field and collapsed in a convulsion. He steadily became more erratic, demanding, mentally unbalanced. Doctors, finding no cause, were mystified. His parents took him to hospitals in Nashville, Louisville, New York, and Mayo's in Rochester, Minn. He had to be kept in padded cells or closely guarded. The final diagnosis was dementia praecox, and it was hopeless.

Providentially, the parents placed him in the hands of a local physician who, unknown to them, had heard about

Edgar Cayce. He secretly obtained a reading. "Yes, we have the body," the sleeping seer said. "His brain is on fire. The convolutions in his brain are all red—red as fire. His mind is distorted. In a very short time, unless something is done, he will be a raving maniac. It dates away back —away back, away back." He prescribed a highly potent and dangerous drug. "Specific treatment", he said, "put to the limit."

The doctor began administrating it in ascending doses; 10 drops in the morning, 11 at noon, 12 at night—then 13, 14, 15, up to 20—then back drop by drop to 10. There was no response. A second bottle, then a third; he got up to 60 drops, more than was safe. Three weeks passed.

Then suddenly one morning the youth came calmly down the stairs. "Good morning, Mummy," he said as he used to. "What's for breakfast?" He was fully recovered.

"I got all the credit!" the doctor later recalled. "Cayce just couldn't be mentioned in that day and time!"

Often homespun and unorthodox treatments were advised. Here is a typical extract taken from the Foundation's files. This man was a Catholic priest living in Canada. He had suffered from epileptic attacks for many years. Like most of the others, Cayce knew nothing of him not stated in his letter requesting the reading.

"In making applications for eradicating the causes then, we would apply each evening, for two evenings, the heavy castor oil packs; at least three thicknesses of heavy flannel, wrung out in castor oil, as hot as the body can stand same, and placed over the lower portion of the liver, gall duct and caecum area—this extending, of course, to the umbilical centre. Let these remain for one hour at each application, keeping the packs hot by wringing out the castor oil two or three times during the application.

"After the two days of applying the packs, we would begin then with the osteopathic adjustments—with particular reference to a subluxation as will be found indicated in the lower portion of the ninth dorsal centre—or ninth, tenth, and eleventh. Coordinate such corrections with the lumbar axis and the upper dorsal and cervical centres."

The priest later signed a statement that his attacks had ceased and he was apparently completely and permanently cured.

There are hundreds of similar cases in the Virginia Beach files documented by affidavits, statements, letters from attending doctors, hospitals, and the patients themselves.

Less publicized were Cayce's clairvoyant abilities in the waking state. He loved to play games of all kinds, but peculiarly preferred those based on pure luck, rather than mental exercise. One evening in a bridge game he didn't want to play, he demonstrated that he could read every card in an opponent's hand. The strange gift took all the fun out of such games.

He could also see auras—colours emanating from people's heads and shoulders. Once, he became concerned about a woman in the neighbourhood who had no aura, and his instinct proved correct. A few days after noticing this, the woman died. Another time he passed a woman he didn't know on the post office steps. Suddenly he stopped, turned, and hurried after her. Touching her on the elbow, he said, "Please don't go on an auto ride today!" She stared at him, and he retired in embarrassment. That evening she found her way to his house. Because of his warning she had cancelled a ride with a friend that day. The friend had gone alone and had a serious accident. The woman wanted to express her gratitude to a man she didn't know. To a young basketball player he accurately forecast how many goals he would score that evening.

One day while taking down a reading, Cayce's stenographer noticed her little nephew playing dangerously close to a lake back of the Cayce home in Virginia Beach. Frightened, she could hardly contain herself. Cayce, asleep on the couch, stopped in the middle of the reading and said, "Go and get the child." When she returned, he picked up where they'd left off.

A water dowser, he advised a Boy Scout troop where to dig a well—32 feet deep. They struck water at 32½ feet.

Cayce once greeted a complete stranger by name. Curious, the man, a local bank official, questioned him, and, intrigued, invited him to lunch. During the meal, Cayce proved his clairvoyance by correctly writing down the combination to the bank safe. The banker was speechless when he read it.

One time Cayce asked a friend, Marsden Godfrey, if he

could drive him to New York. Godfrey begged off; he was exceptionally busy at work and knew there was no use in asking his boss.

"You go ahead and ask, anyway," Edgar told him. He did, and was shocked when his supervisor said it was all right. When Godfrey drove up to the Cayce home, Edgar was standing out front, all ready to go.

Years later, after he had retired, Godfrey told the story to his boss, who remembered the episode explicitly. "I wondered after you left what in the world made me let you go! I needed you badly at the time. You and Cayce shouldn't have done that to me."

But Cayce never liked to use his strange powers in this way, and was always reluctant to do so.

But in 1923 a startling new kind of reading was discovered. Cayce was operating a photographic studio in Selma, Alabama, when one day a well-to-do printer from Dayton, Ohio, walked in. His name was Arthur Lammers, and neither he nor the members of his family were sick. His hobby was metaphysical philosophy, and what he wanted to know was far beyond the range of Edgar's normal thinking.

"What is the meaning of life?" he asked. "What is the origin of talents, abilities, faults, and virtues? How can the inequality of men be explained?"

Cayce was puzzled. He had never thought about such questions.

"You ought to find out about these things", Lammers said. "What is the real nature of man? What is the meaning of birth and death? Why are we here? Haven't you ever asked any of these questions?"

"No," Edgar replied.

"Heavens, man", Lammers exclaimed. "If there's any way to find out about the riddles of life it's through the readings! Come up to Dayton as my guest—I promise you'll be a wiser man when we're through."

Cayce never made any promises about the readings, but he accepted the invitation, and that was the beginning of the metaphysical thought to eventually emerge from 2,500 "Life" readings, as distinguished from the "Physical" readings he had previously been giving.

It was an enormous plan, and it sounded both plausible and fantastic to many. For Cayce, it was the beginning of another period of tortuous self-doubt. Brought up in an atmosphere of strict, orthodox, Protestant Christianity, he was uninformed on the other great religions of the world and their similarities with his own. What the readings now said seemed foreign to everything he had been taught and had been teaching in his Sunday school classes for many years. The essential principles of the great religions, said the readings, were nevertheless all the same—they were only clothed in different garments.

Cayce withheld judgment on the point for a long time. In the end he and those close to the work came to accept reincarnation. It was unprovable of course, but in provable instances the readings had shown themselves to be honest if not infallible. The answers were consistent; one rarely contradicted another even when taken years apart while he was discussing widely different subjects.

For a Life reading—a sort of character and vocational analysis—the suggestions to the sleeping psychic were different. The conductor would say, "You will give the relation of this entity and the universe, giving the conditions which are as personalities, latent and exhibited in the present life; also the former appearances in the earth plane, giving the time, place and the name, and that in each life which built or retarded the development for the entity; giving the abilities of the present entity and that to which it may attain, and how. You will answer the questions as they are asked."

After a while—sometimes so long a time it would seem he had not heard the suggestions—Cayce would repeat the name and address. Then he would say, "Yes—we have the records, we are given the records here of that entity now known as or called _____." He would then discuss the faults and virtues of the personality, its former three or four most important incarnations in the earth, and its present abilities and talents.

One man was told that he had served in the Confederate Army as Barnett A. Seay, and that his record could still be found in the archives of the Virginia State Historical Library in Richmond. The man made a trip to Richmond, and there, after considerable search, found the muster role containing the name of Barnett A. Seay. He had volunteered as a flag bearer in Lee's Army of Virginia in 1861 at the age of 21.

Many of the Life readings in the Cayce files show past incarnations during the Civil War period, and this could be an explanation for the recent phenomenal interest in that subject. Civil War books and stories have been attracting attention undreamed of twenty years ago. No one knows why. Could those people now be incarnating in the U.S.? Are they anti-war?

A woman was told her morbid fear of large bodies of water was due to death by drowning in a past life. A New York entertainer of great charm and personality was told that he had earned it by his unselfish efforts as a pioneer in the early West. Much of this type of information could not be proved, but the deformed and the handicapped had a new understanding of the possible causes of their otherwise unexplained deficiencies.

Eventually, somebody thought to ask the sleeping Cayce where he was getting his information. He gave two sources his mind apparently succeeded in tapping. One was the unconscious or subconscious mind of the subject himself; the other was what was called the universal memory of nature, Jung's Collective Unconscious, or the Akashic Records. This is the "Recording Angel", or the "Book of Life".

Say the Cayce records: "Edgar Cayce's mind is amenable to suggestion, the same as all other subconscious minds; but in addition thereto, it has the power to interpret to the objective mind of others what it acquires from the subconscious minds of other individuals of the same kind. The subconscious forgets nothing. The conscious mind receives the impressions from without and transfers all thought to the subconscious, where it remains even though the conscious be destroyed" as in death.

It is not surprising that the subconscious mind would retain its past experiences, or that it would be aware of the malfunctions of its own physical body in sickness. This is partially in line with the views of modern psychiatry.

But, also say the readings, "The information as obtained and given by this body (E.C.) is gathered from the sources from which the suggestion may derive its information. In this state the conscious mind becomes subjugated to the subconscious, the superconscious, or soul mind, and may and does communicate with like minds, and the subconscious or soul force becomes *universal*. From any subconscious mind information may be obtained either from this plane or from the *impression* as left by the individuals *that have gone before*. As we see a mirror directly reflecting that which is before it—it is not the object itself, but that reflected."

This is a new idea. If it is true, then Cayce's mind was able to tap the mass of knowledge possessed by millions of other subconscious minds, including those who have passed over to the spiritual, cosmic realms in death. This would be an almost unlimited source of wisdom, since it was universal and Cayce was unhindered by time and space. Upon this "Akashic record" is supposedly registered every sound, every thought, every vibration since the beginning of time. Cayce, then, was no "Medium". When this idea first appeared in a reading, few, including Cayce, could believe it. Science knew nothing of any such etheric substance. His critics proclaimed him to be everything from a quack doctor to a religious heretic. He was arrested in New York for "fortune telling" without a licence. When the judge learned Edgar's story, he dismissed the case.

Newspaper headlines left him as unmoved as offers of fame and large sums of money. Although he never earned more than a modest living at best, he turned down all efforts by others to commercialize on the readings. Desperately poor at times, he once flatly refused an offer of $1,000 a day to go on the stage. Simple in his tastes, he was an expert fisherman and a horrible golfer. He loved to talk about the Bible and would preach a sermon at the drop of a word. Yet he was not averse to taking an occasional drink and was a chain-smoker of cigarettes.

With the growing publicity came an increase in the number of requests for readings. Edgar felt compelled to give up his now thriving photography studio in Selma and devote full time to the readings. A moderate fee, usually $10, was charged, but if he felt the person was unable to pay, or failed to enclose the amount in their letter, he never insisted upon it.

In 1925, when Cayce was 48, he took the advice of the readings and moved to Virginia Beach. People with money and influence were attracted to his work. The Association of National Investigators, Inc. was formed in 1927 to carry on psychic research. In 1928, Morton Blumenthal, a wealthy New Yorker, built and furnished the Cayce Hospital. In 1930, Atlantic University, with his backing, opened with Dr. William M. Brown, former professor of psychology at Washington and Lee University, as president. The magazine, *New Tomorrow,* began publication the same year.

Edgar was elated with the rapid growth. He'd never had it so good. Then the roof fell in. The stock market crash, which he predicted, caught up with Blumenthal and wiped him out, and with him, the Association, the hospital, the university, and the magazine. All Cayce had left was the readings and a solid core of "believers". There were lean years after that, but he held on. Then came World War II. A national magazine ran an article titled, *Miracle Man of Virginia Beach,* and Edgar was swamped with an avalanche of 25,000 requests for readings. By 1944 he was a year behind in appointments and suffering from over-exertion and edema of the lungs.

A stroke confined him to bed. Now 67, he never recovered. His last reading, given for himself, was not followed by the doctors in charge. On January 3rd, 1945, Edgar Cayce passed over to the other side. No man ever left the world a stranger legacy.

From the wealth of material in the Cayce files grew The Association for Research and Enlightenment, Inc., The Edgar Cayce Foundation and its affiliated organization, The A.R.E. Press. The Foundation is presently engaged in correlating and cross-indexing the 14,246 readings for ready reference. The subject matter almost blankets the field of human thought; from the value of peanuts to the meaning of the Resurrection; from how to get rid of pinworms to the Last Supper. The Foundation is under the direction of Hugh Lynn, Edgar's oldest son, a scholarly looking man with a Southern accent. He did not inherit his father's psychic ability.

The Association for Research and Enlightenment is an open-membership, non-profit organization chartered under the laws of the Commonwealth of Virginia to carry on psychic research. It is devoted to the study of the readings and conducts numerous experiments in psychic phenomena. It also cooperates with and encourages investigation by qualified persons in the fields of medicine, psychology, and theology. The active membership of the A.R.E. as it is usually called, is made up of people of all religious faiths and many nationalities, including foreign countries. Strangely, they all seem able to reconcile their religious faiths with the metaphysical philosophy emerging from the Cayce readings. They come from all walks of life; there are doctors, lawyers, ministers, artists, businessmen, school teachers, students, working people, housewives. The only requirements for membership are an open mind and a nominal fee of $15 a year.

The Association, governed by a board of trustees, carries on a large programme. It regularly sponsors lecture tours to all parts of the country, participates in radio and TV interviews, and annually holds one congress and numerous conferences at the Virginia Beach Headquarters. Regional conferences are also held in New York, Dallas, Phoenix, Denver, Los Angeles, and other large cities.

The A.R.E. operates a lending library of ten thousand volumes on psychic phenomena, metaphysics, and related subjects, one of the largest of its kind in the world. It also has a tape library of American and English lecturers whose names are well known in the field of parapsychology. In addition, it conducts summer youth and family camps, an abstracting service for requests on specific subjects, and numerous studies along the lines suggested by the readings. Medical research is being carried on by interested doctors, and a clinic has been established in Phoenix.

There are also regional A.R.E. Centres, located in New York, Los Angeles, and Phoenix. These carry on active programmes of their own. Scattered across the country are over a thousand Study Groups devoted to the personal application of the spiritual concepts propounded in the readings. The membership, some 13,000 in number, receives a monthly news bulletin and a periodical, The *A.R.E. Journal*, from the Virginia Beach headquarters.

The Edgar Cayce Publishing Co., now called the A.R.E. Press, was formed soon after Cayce's death to meet the public demand for material from the readings. Although personal readings could no longer be obtained, new people continued to join out of interest in those already on file. Material on a variety of subjects has been extracted from the readings and put in pamphlet form: the Nativity, the Revelation, drugless therapy, spiritual healing, diet and food values, psychosomatic medicine, marriage, child training, the meaning and interpretation of dreams, meditation, the Bible.

Many of these are highly controversial, but the Cayce discourses supply some provocative and often convincing answers to questions that otherwise remain unanswered. Spirit communication for instance is within the realm of possibility, say the readings, but it is not encouraged. There is little to be gained from it; just because Grandpa has passed over to the other side doesn't mean he is suddenly endowed with the wisdom!

Such morsels as these sometimes occur: Don't put cream in your coffee, mixed together, they are harmful to the body; one leaf of lettuce will kill a thousand pinworms; when the devil can't get a man any other way he sends a woman after him; so live that you can tell anybody where to get off—but see to it that they get off at the same place!

The A.R.E. has a mailing list of over 100,000 persons interested in material out of the Cayce files. It also supplies free material to inquirers, newcomers, the curious, the serious. Every mail brings requests from all parts of the country, and sometimes as far away as India, Japan and Europe.

The Edgar Cayce Foundation and its affiliated organizations occupy a large, rambling, three-story frame building of shore architecture. Standing on the highest elevation at Virginia Beach, the building and grounds take up a full city block and face towards the Atlantic Ocean, a block away.

Even the location of the headquarters has an eerie story behind it. In the nineteen-twenties, Cayce's readings repeatedly stated that he should move to Virginia Beach. He had long dreamed of having a hospital where patients could be treated in strict accordance with the readings. Here, they insisted, a hospital could be built, and furthermore,

Cayce should be "near the water", which would be conducive to his work. The best location was just beyond the city limits on the north side of town. This was an ideal spot and direction of growth for the city.

When Cayce arrived in Virginia Beach, then little more than a fishing village, he found the opposite to be true. The expansion was to the south. New subdivisions of home and business sites were being heavily promoted. Some construction was already under way. The north side of town was ignored. With the financial backing of Blumenthal, the hospital was built in 1928 on a north-side site suggested by the readings—and against the advice of the realtors and business men of the community. The location was all wrong.

But in a short time the development to the south died a sudden death. Large scale construction never materialized. Lots and streets remained staked out and vacant. For many years now the expansion has been to the north. The city has grown around the hospital and far beyond it. The site, on the highest elevation in the town, is now the most beautiful and desirable in the community.

Unfortunately, the hospital was not a profit-making institution, and since Cayce himself had no money, the property had to be returned to the backer after the '29 crash. The hospital, which had handled some remarkable cases, was forced to close.

After that debacle, the building was subsequently used as a hotel, a dance hall, gambling casino, nurses' home, private club, art gallery. All of them failed. The place became a jinx and a white elephant; nothing could succeed there. Finally, in 1956, the A.R.E. with the unexpected help of a donor, scraped up a small down payment and purchased the property. The files were moved back to their intended home after twenty-five years.

If the activity today is any indication, they will be there for a long time to come.

SELECTED BIBLIOGRAPHY

Berlitz, Charles. *The Mystery of Atlantis.* New York: Grosset and Dunlap, 1970.

Bushnell, G. H. S. *Peru: Ancient Peoples and Places.* New York: Frederick A. Praeger, 1957.

Ceram, C. W. *Gods, Graves, and Scholars.* New York: Alfred A. Knopf, Inc., 1961.

Cerminara, Gina. *Many Mansions.* New York: William Sloane Associates, 1950; London: Neville Spearman Ltd., 1967.

de la Vega, Garcilaso. *The Incas.* New York: Orion Press, 1961.

de Riencourt, Amaury. *The American Empire.* New York: The Dial Press, 1968.

Deuel, Leo. *Conquistadors Without Swords.* New York: St. Martin's Press, 1967.

Donnelly, Ignatius. *Atlantis, the Antediluvian World.* (Rev.) New York: Harper and Row, 1949.

Ferro, Robert, and Michael Grunly. *Atlantis, the Autobiography of a Search.* New York: Doubleday and Co., 1970.

Fulbright, J. W. *The Pentagon Propaganda Machine.* New York: Liveright Publishing Corp., 1970.

Gann, T. W. F. *Ancient Cities and Modern Tribes.* London: Duckworth, 1926.

Heyerdahl, Thor. *Kon Tiki.* Chicago: Rand McNally, 1950.

Hyams, Edward, and George Ordish. *Last of the Incas.* New York: Simon and Schuster, 1963.

Lundberg, Ferdinand. *The Rich and the Super-Rich.* New York: Lyle Stuart, Inc., 1968.

McGregor, John C. *Southwestern Archaeology.* Urbana, Ill.: University of Illinois Press (Rev.), 1965.

Meriwether, David. *In the Mountains and on the Plains.* Norman, Okla.: University of Oklahoma Press, 1965.

Morley, Sylvanus G. *The Ancient Maya.* Stanford, Calif.: Stanford University Press, 1956.

Mowat, Farley, *Westviking: The Ancient Norse in Greenland and North America*. Boston: Little, Brown and Co., 1965.

Ostrander, Sheila, and Lynn Schroeder. *Psychic Discoveries Behind the Iron Curtain*. Englewood Cliffs, N. J.: Prentice-Hall, Inc., 1970.

Pearson, Drew, and Jack Anderson. *The Case Against Congress*. New York: Simon and Schuster, 1968.

Rowe, John M. *Inca Culture at the Time of the Spanish Conquest*. In Handbook of South American Indians, Smithsonian Inst., Washington, D. C., Bureau of American Ethnology, 1946–1950.

Stephens, John L. *Incidents of Travel in South America*. Vol. 1. New York: Harper and Bros., 1841.

Stephenson, Ian. *Twenty Cases Suggestive of Reincarnation*. New York: American Society for Psychical Research, 1966.

Stern, Jesse. *The Sleeping Prophet*. New York: Doubleday and Co., 1967.

Sugrue, Thomas. *There is a River*. New York: Henry Holt and Co., 1942.

Thompson, Edward H. *People of the Serpent*. Boston: Houghton Mifflin, 1932.

Von Hagen, Victor. *Realm of the Incas*. New York: New American Library, 1957.

Waters, Frank. *Book of the Hopi*. New York: Viking Press, 1963.

Weatherhead, Leslie D. *The Case for Reincarnation*. Surrey, England: M. C. Peto, 1958.

Wise, David, and Thomas B. Ross. *The Invisible Government*. New York: Random House, Inc., 1964.